Essential Guide for
Warehouse Management
using
Microsoft Dynamics AX

2016 Edition

Other Books by Scott Hamilton

Supply Chain Management Using Microsoft Dynamics AX: 2016 Edition,
Visions, Inc. (2016)

Process Manufacturing Using Microsoft Dynamics AX: 2016 Edition,
Visions Inc. (2016)

Warehouse Management Using Microsoft Dynamics AX: 2016 Edition,
Visions Inc. (2016)

Discrete Manufacturing Using Microsoft Dynamics AX 2012,
Visions Inc. (2012)

Food Products Manufacturing Using Microsoft Dynamics AX 2012,
Visions Inc. (2012)

Managing Process Manufacturing Using Microsoft Dynamics AX 2009,
Visions Inc. (2010)

Managing Wholesale Distribution Using Microsoft Dynamics AX 2009,
privately published (2010)

Managing Lean Manufacturing Using Microsoft Dynamics AX 2009,
Visions Inc. (2010)

Managing Your Supply Chain Using Microsoft Dynamics AX 2009,
Printing Arts (2009)

Managing Your Supply Chain Using Microsoft Dynamics AX 4.0,
Printing Arts (2007)

Managing Your Supply Chain Using Microsoft Axapta 3.0, McGraw-Hill (2004)

Managing Your Supply Chain Using Microsoft Navision, McGraw-Hill (2004)

Maximizing Your ERP System, McGraw-Hill (2003)

*Managing Information: How Information Systems Impact Organizational
Strategy* (with Gordon B. Davis), Business One Irwin (1993)

Essential Guide for
Warehouse Management
using
Microsoft Dynamics AX

2016 Edition

Scott Hamilton, Ph.D.

eBook ISBN 978-0-9973071-0-8
Print ISBN 978-0-9973071-1-5

The front cover photo depicts a lightning storm over Death Valley in California, and was taken by the nationally-recognized photographer Doug Peck (www.douglaspeckphotography.com).

Contents

Preface

This book focuses on how Microsoft Dynamics AX supports the basic approach to warehouse management in manufacturing and distribution businesses. It covers the essential capabilities and business processes for warehouse management, and includes the related considerations about transportation, quality and supply chain management. The targeted reader consists of warehouse management professionals that need to initially learn AX.

As an Essential Guide, it represents an abbreviated version of my complete book for *Warehouse Management using Microsoft Dynamics AX: 2016 Edition*. This Essential Guide focuses on topics that apply to both distribution and manufacturing, but skims over the manufacturing-related topics due to book length considerations. These topics are covered in the complete book. The complete book also covers the Advanced WMS approach to warehouse management.

A summary of the warehouse management capabilities within AX are included in two previous books titled *Supply Chain Management using Microsoft Dynamics AX: 2016 Edition* and *Process Manufacturing using Microsoft Dynamics AX: 2016 Edition*. These previous books focused on discrete and process manufacturing/ distribution respectively.

The book contents cover two major options currently available for using AX, which can be labeled "Dynamics AX 2012 R3" and the "new Dynamics AX". The two options provide the same warehouse management functionality with some slight differences, so that the book contents apply to both options.

A trail guide and topographic maps provide essential information when exploring any unknown territory. They identify the most important features of the landscape and provide insights about key considerations and trail variations. Similar essentials apply to those exploring the use of an ERP system to run their business. This Essential Guide identifies the most important features of the embedded conceptual models and business processes related to basic warehouse management using AX, and provides insights about key considerations and variations.

Many people helped in completing this book. They included Deb Skoog, Elise Kling Marty and Sandra Krzyzaniak in preparing the book. In addition, many people contributed insights and feedback to the previous books which acted as the source material for this essential guide.

The book reflects my interpretation of how to use Microsoft Dynamics AX. Errors of omission and commission, and any misunderstandings, are hopefully minimized.[1] Corrections and suggestions are welcome, as well as additional case study examples. Please send to ScottHamiltonPhD@aol.com.

Each day of writing was started with the following prayer:

> Creator of all things, give me a sharp sense of understanding, a retentive memory, and the ability to grasp things correctly and fundamentally. Grant me the talent of being exact in my explanations, and the ability to express myself with thoroughness and charm. Point out the beginning, direct the progress, and help in the completion.

---

[1] The book is for information purposes only. The author, publisher and Microsoft make no warranties, expressed or implied, in the presentation of information.

Chapter 1

Introduction

A primary challenge for many manufacturing and distribution firms involves effective implementation and use of an ERP system for managing their supply chain, especially for warehouse management. Learning the capabilities of your ERP system provides a foundation for effective usage, and re-thinking previous ways of doing business. When initially learning an ERP system, the sheer amount of functionality can be daunting, and make the task difficult and time-consuming. The learning curve can be shortened with a guide book that covers the essential topics and processes for running the business. A guide book can help you learn the vocabulary about embedded conceptual models, and enhance the hands-on experience of system usage and navigational details. Each ERP system has its own vocabulary, conceptual models and navigational details, including Microsoft Dynamics AX.[1]

This book focuses on how Dynamics AX supports the basic approach to warehouse management in manufacturing and distribution businesses. It provides an overview of the essential business processes and capabilities, and covers the embedded conceptual models that ultimately shape your vocabulary for describing system usage. The targeted reader consists of warehouse management professionals that need to initially learn AX.

This Essential Guide represents an abbreviated version of my complete book for "Warehouse Management using Microsoft Dynamics AX: 2016 Edition". It focuses on topics that apply to both distribution and manufacturing, but skims over the manufacturing-related topics due to book length considerations. These topics are covered in the complete book.

The book contents cover two major options currently available for using AX, which can be labeled "Dynamics AX 2012 R3" and the "new Dynamics AX". The two options provide the same supply chain management functionality with some slight differences, so that the book contents apply to both options. The

---

[1] Dynamics AX is a registered trademark of Microsoft. This book employs the term "AX" for short.

book identifies the slight differences such as the variations in user experience and the workspace capabilities. Beneath these look and feel changes, the two options share the same embedded conceptual models and business processes.

This chapter starts with suggestions for the targeted reader, and describes the scope of book topics. It also covers several aspects of terminology and highlights the use of business process modeling (BPM) diagrams as a learning tool. These considerations are reflected in the following sections within this chapter.

1. Suggestions for the Targeted Reader
2. Scope of Book Topics and Prior Research
3. Terminology Used in the Book
4. Variations in the User Experience and the use of Workspaces
5. Business Process Modeling (BPM) Diagrams as Learning Tools
6. Baseline Model of Operations
7. Summary of Case Studies

1.1 Suggestions for the Targeted Reader

The targeted reader consists of professionals that need to initially learn Dynamics AX and the basic approach to warehouse management in distribution and manufacturing businesses. In many cases, these professionals comprise the project team responsible for the initial implementation. In other cases, they may need to learn AX because of a change in positions or job responsibilities. Prospective users (and AX consultants) may also want to initially learn AX. In addition, many people with some AX experience may want to confirm and extend their AX knowledge, or selectively learn a topic. Figure 1.1 summarizes these learning objectives.

Figure 1.1 Suggestions for the Targeted Reader

Learning Objective	Estimated Pages
Initially Learn AX and Basic Warehouse Management	80-100
Extend/Confirm existing AX knowledge	
Selectively Learn AX Capabilities	

The objective to initially learn AX can benefit from an overview of the essential business processes and capabilities. The sequence of topics starts with the fundamentals of the basic approach to warehouse management. This includes the significance of Inventory Status, the definition of inventory locations within a warehouse, and the basic inventory transactions such as adjustments and transfers. The sequence continues with several types of warehouse-related transactions, including purchase order receiving, sales order picking/shipping, and transfer order picking/shipping and receiving. The final topics cover several considerations about transportation and quality management. The book chapters reflect this sequence, as shown in Figure 1.2.

Figure 1.2 Organization of Book Chapters

Chapter	Topics
2	Fundamentals of the Basic Approach to Warehouse Management
3	Purchase Order Receiving
4	Sales Order Picking/Shipping
5	Transfer Order Picking/Shipping
6	Transfer Order Receiving
7	Basics of Transportation
8	Quality Management Considerations

For each type of transaction, the explanation covers a basic model of the business process, the related constructs and their life cycles, the reversing transactions, and the major variations. The typical steps and role responsibilities for a business process are illustrated using BPM diagrams. The basic model provides a baseline for explaining these variations, thereby supporting a "+1" learning approach.

Warehouse management has a larger context of supply chain management (SCM). My explanation of warehouse management capabilities within AX assumes some level of knowledge about the essential SCM capabilities within AX. A separate book provides the "Essential Guide to Supply Chain Management using Microsoft Dynamics AX: 2016 Edition".

1.2 Scope of Book Topics and Prior Research

This essential guide focuses on warehouse management topics that apply to distribution and manufacturing companies. It skims over or excludes several topics related to manufacturing, and these topics are covered in the complete book about warehouse management. It also skims over or excludes several other topics, as described in Appendix A about the scope of book topics. This appendix also describes the scope of prior research.

The selection of topics for this essential guide were shaped by my experience in teaching SCM professionals across the past three decades. This includes teaching new users (and experienced users) as part of consulting engagements with several hundred firms, and also teaching SCM topics as part of executive seminars, APICS certification classes, MBA courses, user group sessions, and AX training courses. The topics were also shaped by my experience in writing multiple books about SCM using AX.

1.3 Terminology Used in the Book

The terminology associated with many aspects of warehouse management can vary widely between companies and ERP systems. It is often difficult to clearly understand the meaning of a term -- such as inventory status, reservations and shipments -- without a lengthy discussion about its significance.

As much as possible, this book consistently uses the same terminology to describe the conceptual models and software functionality within AX. In most cases, the book's terminology reflects the names employed by the AX software, such as the names of forms and fields. However, it sometimes reflects generally accepted terms or alternative phrasing to clarify understanding.

One difficulty in terminology stems from the book's attempt to explain two different options for using AX, consisting of AX 2012 R3 version and the new Dynamics AX. The embedded conceptual models and business processes within the two options are fundamentally the same for warehouse management topics, but there are slight changes. A comprehensive list of these changes was not available prior to book publications. The book uses the new term when known, otherwise it uses the terminology from AX 2012 R3.

1.4 Variations in the User Experience and the use of Workspaces

This book focuses on the embedded conceptual models and business processes within standard AX. The user experience and navigational details may differ -- whether using customized forms, workspaces, web-based applications, or hand-held devices -- but the embedded conceptual models and business processes still apply. This section summarizes the variations in user experience and the use of workspaces.

Variations of the User Experience The standard menu structure and user-defined favorites provide commonly used approaches for navigation. When using the new Dynamics AX, the links within workspaces provide another approach for navigating to commonly used tasks. An additional approach – termed "search for a page" – enables you to specify the desired topic, review a list of applicable forms, and then navigate to a selected form.

Use of Workspaces Workspaces represent one variation in the user experience when using the new Dynamics AX. Workspaces provide an aggregation of tasks related to a specific role. Almost half of the 30+ currently available workspaces apply to SCM-related topics. Two workspaces apply to the basic approach to warehouse management, as described below.

◆ *Cost Administration Workspace.* This workspace includes links to key reports/inquiries about inventory accounting, such as inventory value statements, inventory aging, standard cost transactions, and calculation of ABC classifications.

◆ *Cost Analysis Workspace.* This workspace summarizes inventory turns and inventory accuracy (with drill down to those items with low turns or accuracy) as well as inventory value (with segmentation by item group and also total inventory value over time). The links provide access to key reports/inquiries about inventory accounting, such as inventory value statements, inventory aging, and calculation of ABC classifications.

1.5 Business Process Modeling (BPM) Diagrams as a Learning Tool

One of the book's primary objectives consists of learning the embedded conceptual models and business processes within standard AX. In many implementations, these business processes can help the project team gain an overall understanding of system usage and each team member's roles, enabling them to envision new business practices and the real need for customizations. Many of the chapters include Business Process Modeling (BPM) diagrams about basic business processes. These basic processes provide the foundation for more extended explanations and for covering major variations. BPM diagrams are primarily used as a learning tool within this book, and my diagrams do not adhere exactly to the BPM standards. The diagrams employ a limited number of symbols to keep things simple. For example, three symbols are used to denote "And", "Or" and "Any, None, or All". A fourth symbol for an "Event" indicates an automatic action within AX, which helps explain some of the behind-the-scenes functionality. The BPM diagrams indicate a sub-process using a bold border for the activity.

1.6 Baseline Model of Operations

A baseline model of operations represents the common use of Dynamics AX and dominant business practices within many manufacturing and distribution businesses. It provides a foundation for simplified explanations about how to use Dynamics AX to manage the business, and for explaining variations to the baseline model. In summary, the baseline model focuses on a single AX company with one or more AX sites (and their related AX warehouses) with standard products identified by an item number. Inventory is tracked by site, warehouse and bin location, with inventory replenishment logic at the site/warehouse level. The following points provide more detailed explanations about the baseline model of operations for the basic approach to warehouse management.

Single Company and AX instance The baseline model consists of a single company using a single AX instance. Some scenarios involve multiple companies within one instance and possible partitioning of these companies within the database. A multicompany supply chain is treated as a variation to the baseline model.

Multiple Inventory Locations Identified by an AX site and AX Warehouse Each physical location is typically identified by an AX site and an associated value for a "site" financial dimension. The site-specific financial dimension supports financial reports by site. Each AX site has one or more AX warehouses. Each AX warehouse has one or more bin locations, although use of bin locations is not mandatory. The definition and use of warehouse locations differ significantly between the basic and advanced approach to warehouse management.

Material Items Identified by Item Number Material items are identified by an item number. In some cases, an item may be identified by an item number and one or more additional fields termed variant codes, as illustrated in Case 3.3. In other cases, a product configurator can result in the creation of a configuration ID for the item number. These are treated as variations to the baseline model of operations.

Batch and/or Serial Numbers for a Material Item The use of batch and/or serial numbers is treated as a variation to the baseline model.

1.7 Summary of Case Studies

Case studies illustrate how the AX software functionality applies to many different scenarios in manufacturing and distribution. Each chapter includes case studies applicable to the topic, and a complete list of case studies is provided at the end of the book. Additional case studies are included in the complete book.

Chapter 2

Fundamentals of the Basic Inventory Approach

Several fundamentals of the Basic Inventory approach provide the foundation for explaining business processes in subsequent chapters. These fundamentals include the key setup information such as the definition of a warehouse and its locations, and the item-related policies for warehouse management. They also include basic inventory transactions such as transfers and adjustments. These considerations are reflected in the following sections within the chapter.

1. Major Options for Warehouse Management
2. Significance of the Inventory Status
3. Summary of Warehouse-Related Transactions
4. Basic Inventory Transactions
5. Define a Non-WMS Warehouse and its Locations
6. Define Item-Related Policies for Warehouse Management
7. Calculate Space Utilization for a Non-WMS Warehouse

2.1 Major Options for Warehouse Management

The various warehouse management options have been called many different names, but they boil down to two major options. For simplicity's sake, one major option can be termed the "Basic Inventory approach" or the "basic approach" for short. The second major option can be termed the "Advanced WMS approach" or the "advanced approach" for short. We will use the shortened terms moving forward.

The two major options are differentiated by a warehouse policy and an item-related policy about "use warehouse management processes." The advanced approach only applies to warehouse transactions for a WMS-enabled item at a WMS-enabled warehouse, whereas the basic approach applies to the other combinations of these two policies. Figure 2.1 summarizes these key policies and the two major options for warehouse management (identified as Option #1 and #2). It also identifies the terminology about items and warehouses, such as a WMS-enabled item, a WMS-enabled warehouse, and a non-WMS warehouse.

Figure 2.1   Major Options for Warehouse Management

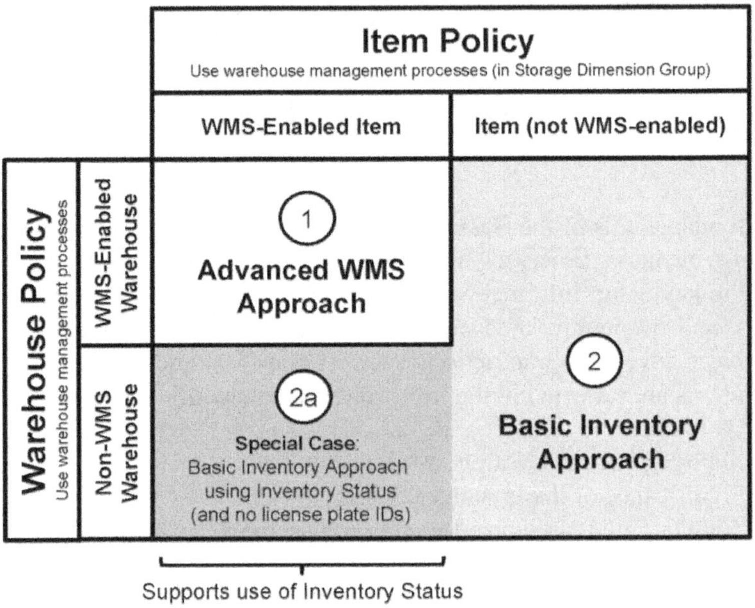

The two major options are reflected in the AX user documentation, which differentiates various topics as applicable to "features in the warehouse management module" versus "features in the inventory management module." The basic approach has some unique constructs and functionality as does the advanced approach, and the two options also share a high degree of common functionality.

The basic approach typically applies to a warehouse (or company) that does not have sophisticated requirements for sales order picking/shipping, and does not require tracking of palletized inventory. Inventory within the warehouse is typically tracked by piece rather than by pallet. In addition, the basic approach does not support out-of-the box mobile device transactions. If needed, third-party applications supporting mobile device transactions can be used with the basic approach.   The basic approach supports simple, order-based picking for sales orders and transfer orders, and it can also support the wave-picking concept for these orders.

A firm with simplistic needs for warehouse management can start with out-of-the-box functionality in the basic approach (Case 2.1) and implement mobile device transactions via third-party applications (Case 2.2). A firm may also employ the basic approach for smaller sites, remote locations or subcontractor locations while using the advanced approach at larger warehouses (Case 2.3). In addition, a given warehouse may start with the basic approach as an interim step to the advanced approach (Case 2.4).

Case 2.1: Simplistic Needs for Warehouse Transactions   A
manufacturing and distribution company had simplistic needs for warehouse transactions.   They implemented the Basic Inventory approach at the various warehouses since they did not require the additional functionality within the Advanced WMS approach.   In addition, they were happy with screen-based approaches for entering warehouse transactions, and did not yet perceive a need for data collection via mobile devices.

Case 2.2: Support Mobile Devices Using 3rd-Party Applications A
manufacturing and distribution company was implementing the Basic Inventory approach at the various warehouses since they did not require the additional functionality within the Advanced WMS approach. This meant they could not use the out-of-the-box mobile device transactions, so they employed a third-party solution for these data collection purposes.[1] The solution supported all variations of transactions within the basic approach, and provided a simpler user interface for the mobile device transactions (relative to the out-of-the-box mobile device transactions).

Case 2.3: Manage Inventory at Off-site Warehouses   A
manufacturer/distributor employed the Advanced WMS functionality and mobile device transactions at their main warehouse. However, they also needed to track inventory and report transactions at their off-site warehouses that represented subcontractors and remote locations. They used simple inventory transactions for many situations, such as reporting purchase order receipts of supplied material at a subcontractor, or transfer order receipts at a remote warehouse. In some situations, they selectively employed capabilities within the Basic Inventory approach, such as generating picking lists for all sales order shipments from a subcontractor or remote warehouse.

---

[1] The RF-SMART capabilities support mobile device transactions for the Basic Inventory approach. See www.rfsmart.com for more information.

Case 2.4: Interim Step to Using Advanced WMS Approach   A manufacturer/distributor was implementing AX with a two-phased approach for warehouse management.   For Phase 1, they employed the simpler Basic Inventory approach, which would serve as an interim step before implementing the Advanced WMS approach.   More specifically, they defined items as WMS-enabled and initially defined non-WMS warehouses and their locations.   For Phase 2, they would define another set of WMS-enabled warehouses with the exact same location identifiers.   When cutting over to Phase 2, the inventory in their previous warehouses will be transferred to the corresponding WMS-enabled warehouse and location.   In addition, the demands and supply orders would be updated to reflect the change to WMS-enabled warehouses.

2.2 Significance of the Inventory Status

A special case of the Basic Inventory approach—identified as Option #2a in Figure 2.1—can take advantage of the capabilities related to Inventory Status. The Inventory Status capabilities only apply to WMS-enabled items.   License plates can also apply to WMS-enabled items, but only for transactions at WMS-enabled warehouses.   License plate information does not apply for transactions at a non-WMS warehouse.

Inventory Status has a broad range of potential uses, and its capabilities are largely determined by user-defined values.   At its simplest, a single value can be used for Inventory Status so that it provides no additional capabilities.

Most scenarios employ multiple user-defined values to support requirements for quality, warehousing, and other areas of the business.   For example, one value typically indicates good inventory, such as a value of *Available* or *Good*.   One or more values can be defined and designated as blocked in order to prevent usage of inventory with the assigned value.   Examples of these user-defined values include *Blocked* or *Damaged*.   Master scheduling logic treats this "blocked" inventory as non-nettable.

The user-defined values can indicate needed action when assigned to existing inventory.   Examples include *Needs-Inspection, Needs-Rework, Return-to-Vendor*, and *To-Be-Scrapped*.   You typically place the inventory in a related location at the same time, such as moving it to a special location when assigning the value *To-Be-Scrapped*.   In the context of these example values, the assigned value indicates the need for a corresponding action to create a quality order, rework order, purchase order return, or an inventory adjustment.

The inspection requirements for a purchased item can be identified by the Inventory Status capabilities, thereby providing an alternative to the use of Quality Associations. For example, the value of *Needs-Inspection* (or its equivalent) can be assigned to an item and a supplying vendor so that the value is automatically inherited by a purchase order line and communicated to receiving clerks at the time of reporting arrival.

The user-defined values can also indicate the grade or condition of inventory, which may or may not affect sales or purchase prices. Examples include *Off-Spec, Refurbished* or *Used.*

A value for Inventory Status must be assigned to orders, typically with a value of *Good* or its equivalent in most scenarios. It can be changed during the receiving process for purchased or manufactured items (or for RMA receipts), such as changing the value from *Good* to *Needs-Inspection.* It can also be changed by quality orders, such as automatically changing the value to *Needs-Rework* or *To-be-Scrapped* when validation failure occurs. In a similar fashion, passing the validation can automatically update the value to *Good.* The value for existing inventory can also be changed when needed. More comprehensive explanations about the significance of Inventory Status are provided in the complete book about warehouse management.

2.3 Summary of Warehouse-Related Transactions

The explanation of the warehouse management approach is organized around warehouse-related transactions. These are summarized in Figure 2.2. Each type of transaction is covered in subsequent chapters in terms of an example business process. The figure identifies the section numbers describing each business process.

Other types of inventory transactions are not considered because of book length considerations. Examples include transactions for projects and service orders, retail-specific transactions related to stores, and kanban transactions for lean manufacturing.

2.4 Basic Inventory Transactions

The basic inventory transactions include transfers, adjustments, and cycle counts. These basic transactions and some related inquiries/analyses are summarized in Figure 2.3, which provides an organizing focus for further explanation.

Figure 2.2   Examples of Warehouse-Related Transactions

Type of Transaction		Example Process
Basic Inventory Transactions	Inventory Transfer (Movement)	Section 2.3
	Inventory Adjustment - Out	
	Inventory Adjustment - In	
	Quantity Adjustment (Count)	
	Cycle Count	
Quality	Change Inventory Status	
	Quarantine Order	Section 8.3
Purchase Order	Purchase Order Arrival	Section 3.1
	Purchase Order Return	Section 3.9
Sales Order	Sales Order Picking/Shipping	Section 4.1
	RMA Arrival	
Transfer Order	Transfer Order Picking/Shipping	Section 5.1
	Transfer Order Arrival	Section 6.1
Production Order	Production Order Picking	
	Production Order Receiving	

Figure 2.3   Summary of Basic Inventory Transactions

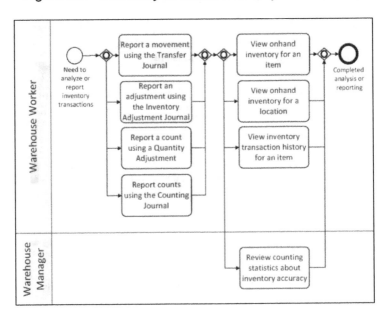

Report Movements Using the Transfer Journal   Inventory movements between locations can be recorded in a transfer journal. Each transfer journal has a system-assigned identifier, and consists of a header and journal line items. Each line minimally identifies an item, quantity, and the old and new locations (identified by site, warehouse and bin). The relevant batch and/or serial number may also need to be identified. The transfer quantity is expressed as a negative, and always reflects the item's inventory UM. The transfer entries can be maintained and printed prior to posting the journal. The status for a Transfer consists of a checkbox labeled Posted, which indicates whether it is open or posted.

A transfer journal typically reflects an immediate transfer of material without a requirement for tracking in transit inventory. For example, a transfer journal may be used to move material between locations in two adjacent warehouses, as illustrated in Case 2.X. Transfer orders should be used when in-transit inventory must be tracked. Subsequent chapters explain the picking/shipping and receiving transactions for transfer orders.

An inventory transfer journal can support the transfer of one variant of an item to another variant, as well as transferring one batch number to another batch number—much like you would transfer inventory from one location to another. A transfer journal also provides an alternative approach for merging different batches of an item.

Report Adjustments Using the Inventory Adjustment Journal
Inventory adjustments can serve a variety of purposes, such as loading initial inventory balances, reporting inventory corrections, and reporting scrap. Adjustments can be recorded using either the Inventory Adjustment Journal or the Movement Journal. The Inventory Adjustment Journal employs a predefined G/L account number for an item's inventory adjustments, whereas a Movement Journal forces you to specify this offsetting G/L account number. Otherwise, these two types of journals are the same in all other respects. Further explanation focuses on just the Inventory Adjustment Journal.

Each Inventory Adjustment journal has a system-assigned identifier, and consists of a header and journal line items. Each line minimally identifies an item, quantity, and location (identified by site, warehouse and bin). The relevant batch and/or serial number may also need to be identified. Items with an actual costing method require an additional entry about the item's unit cost and possible charges. The quantity can be positive or negative, and always reflects the item's inventory UM. The adjustment entries can be maintained and printed prior to posting the journal. The status for an Inventory Adjustment Journal consists of a checkbox labeled Posted, which indicates whether it is open or posted.

Adjustments to an item's inventory quantity can also be recorded using two other approaches described in the next two subsections. These two approaches are termed Quantity Adjustments and Counting Journals.

Report Counts Using Quantity Adjustments   A quantity adjustment is different than using an inventory adjustment journal, and more closely resembles the use of a counting journal. A quantity adjustment can be initiated from on-hand inquiries about an item's inventory or a location's inventory, where you access the Counting form. In either case, you can adjust the quantity for existing inventory or create a new entry to add inventory. Accepting the quantity adjustment(s) will update the inventory and generate a counting history record. You can subsequently view an inquiry of these counting history records, which are not assigned a counting journal number.

Report Counts Using the Counting Journal   A Counting Journal can be used to support cycle counting or physical inventories. Performing a physical inventory count helps ensure valid financial reporting of inventory value. Cycle counting can accomplish the same objective. Each Counting Journal has a system-assigned identifier, and consists of a header and journal line items. Each line minimally identifies an item, quantity, and location (identified by site, warehouse, and bin). The relevant batch and/or serial number may also need to be identified. The status for a Counting Journal consists of a checkbox labeled Posted, which indicates whether it is open or posted.

You can manually or automatically create the journal lines identifying the items to be counted, print the journal as a turnaround document, and then record the counted quantity or the adjustment quantity for each journal line. Posting a counting journal updates the inventory balances. This represents a two-step counting process: one step to identify items in the counting journal, and a second step to post the journal. A companywide policy (embedded in the Inventory and Warehouse Management Parameters form) optionally prevents inventory transactions during the counting process.

◆ *Create Line Items within a Counting Journal.* Automatic creation of journal lines can be based on one or more factors, such as a specified warehouse, a selected range of item numbers or item groups, or the item's cycle counting approach. An item's cycle counting approach (embedded within the Counting Group assigned to an item) typically reflects a periodic interval expressed in calendar days. In this case, you specify a "not counted since" date as the basis for automatically creating journal lines. A further refinement can eliminate any items with no inventory transactions since the last count. Alternatively, the approach can reflect a condition such as on-hand inventory reaching zero or the item's minimum quantity, since this approach minimizes the time and effort for performing a physical count.

◆ *Control Group Method for Cycle Counting.* Some companies employ a control group method in cycle counting, where the same items are counted every day to immediately identify the sources of error. Copying the journal lines from a previous counting journal into the new journal supports the control group method.

◆ *Tag Counting Journal for Physical Inventories.* Some companies employ tags (with pre-assigned numbers) to conduct a physical inventory, typically with handwritten count information about the quantity and location. A separate tag counting journal can be used to record the tag numbers, tag status (used, voided or missing), and the count information, and then analyze missing tag numbers. This tag counting journal represents an approach to tag control. Posting it results in the creation of a counting journal (with journal lines for used tags), which must be posted to update inventory balances.

◆ *View Counting History Records.* You can subsequently view an inquiry of counting history records, which include the identifier of the counting journal.

View Counting Statistics about Inventory Accuracy The warehouse manager can view the Counting Statistics report about the inventory accuracy percentage over a specified date range. The percentage reflects the number of cycle count transactions with a discrepancy divided by the total number of cycle count transactions. The selection criteria for the report typically specify a date range (about counting dates) and summarize the inventory accuracy information by warehouse.

View On-Hand Inventory and Transaction History You can view standardized inquiries about inventory by item or location as well as view transaction history.

2.5 Define a Non-WMS Warehouse and its Locations

Each warehouse has a unique identifier and must be assigned to a site. You designate a non-WMS warehouse by not enabling the *Use Warehouse Management Processes* policy for the warehouse. This policy works in conjunction with a similar item-related policy for determining whether the Basic Inventory approach will be used, as previously described for the major options for warehouse management (Section 2.1). Other warehouse-related information includes its associated bin locations and warehouse type.

Define the Aisles within a Warehouse   One or more aisles within a non-WMS warehouse must be defined prior to defining bin locations, because each bin location must be assigned to an aisle.

Define Bin Locations within a Warehouse   The identifier for a bin location often reflects its coordinates (consisting of an aisle, rack, shelf level and/or bin), but it can reflect another purpose.   The identifier can be manually assigned, or automatically created for specified ranges of aisle, rack, shelf, and bin numbers. You can also copy bin locations from another warehouse.   You can print a barcoded label for each bin location.

A bin must be designated with a location type.   These predefined location types include a bulk location, an inbound dock, an outbound dock, and a picking location.   However, the location type has no significance within the Basic Inventory approach to warehouse management, so that a single location type (such as bulk location) can be assigned to all bin locations.

An item may always be stored in the same bin location.   You designate this "fixed location" by assigning it to the item's default bin locations within a warehouse—one for receipts and one for issues.

As optional information, you can specify the maximum weight and volume for a bin location capacity.   This provides reference information for comparing bin capacity to the weight/volume of items placed in the bin location.   It can also be used to calculate space utilization for a non-WMS warehouse (Section 2.7).

Warehouse Types   A normal warehouse is designated with a warehouse type of main.   Another type of warehouse is needed to support transfer orders, and yet another type is needed to support quarantine orders.

◆   *Transit Warehouse.*   The use of transfer orders requires the definition of a transit warehouse and its assignment to a main warehouse.   A transit warehouse has a separate identifier, a warehouse type of transit, and at least one bin location that acts as a default.   A typical value for this bin location is "InTransit."   You need a minimum of one transit warehouse per site, which can be assigned to each main warehouse within the site.   Alternatively, a transit warehouse can be defined for each main warehouse that acts as a ship-from location for transfer orders.   The different transit warehouses provide more granular visibility of in-transit inventory related to transfer orders.   Subsequent chapters provide further explanation of transfer order transactions (Chapters 5 and 6).

◆ *Quarantine Warehouse.* The use of quarantine orders requires the definition of a quarantine warehouse and its assignment to a main warehouse. A quarantine warehouse has a separate identifier, a warehouse type of quarantine, and its own bin locations. Most situations will employ one quarantine warehouse for each normal warehouse. A subsequent section describes the use of quarantine orders (Section 8.3).

Warehouse-Related Policies A warehouse can have a default bin location that applies to all receipts, and a second default bin location that applies to all issues. These bin locations serve as a default when item-specific defaults are not specified. These default bin locations for a warehouse should only be specified when a single bin location makes sense, such as a single default bin location for a transit warehouse. Two other policies are critical for master scheduling logic.

◆ *Calendar.* A warehouse should have a specified calendar of working hours.

◆ *Nettable vs Non-Nettable Inventory.* Most warehouses will contain nettable inventory. A warehouse can be designated as non-nettable (via the manual planning flag) so that supplies are ignored by master scheduling logic.

2.6 Define Item-Related Policies for Warehouse Management

Several item-related policies must be defined in order to support the Basic Inventory approach to warehouse management.

◆ *Policies within the Storage Dimension Group.* The policies within a Storage Dimension Group identify a WMS-enabled item and also define the applicability of information about site, warehouse, and bin location.

◆ *Policies within the Tracking Dimension Group.* The policies within a Tracking Dimension Group identify the need for tracking serial numbers or batch numbers for an item.

◆ *Unit of Measure (UM) Considerations.* An item can have multiple units of measure and unique UM conversion factors.

◆ *Negative Inventory Policy for Physical On-Hand Inventory.* This policy determines whether negative inventory will be allowed for an item, and is defined within the Item Model Group assigned to the item.

◆ *Fixed Location for an Item.* Sometimes an item is always stored in the same bin location. You designate this "fixed location" by assigning it to the item's default bin locations within a warehouse—one for receipts and one for issues.

2.7 Calculate Space Utilization for a Warehouse

The calculation of space utilization for a non-WMS warehouse (and its associated report) provide aggregate indicators of over- and under-loaded utilization of warehouse capacity. The aggregate indicators are expressed in daily increments over a user-defined time horizon. The space utilization can reflect weight or volume, and the daily increments (expressed as a percentage) provide trending information. This information can highlight intermittent or extended periods of over- or under-loaded utilization so you can plan accordingly.

Calculate Space Utilization   The periodic calculation of space utilization (labeled Schedule Load Utilization) involves several factors as described below.

◆ The maximum weight and volume specified for each bin location's capacity is aggregated into the total capacity for all bin locations within a warehouse.

◆ The weight and volume specified for each item.

◆ The existing inventory of items within bin locations—with weight and volume aggregated into a total for the first daily increment within the time horizon

◆ The expected receipts and issues for an item and warehouse with weight and volume aggregated into a total for each daily increment. The calculation of expected receipts/issues reflects a specified set of master plan data and a specified time horizon.

Review Space Utilization Calculations   The report for space utilization (labeled the Warehouse Load Utilization report) involves several options. The report dialogue provides options about the choice of weight or volume for displaying utilization and the applicable site(s) and warehouse(s). The report displays one line for each warehouse, where the line includes daily increments of space utilization. As an option, you can drill down to the detailed receipts and issues for a selected daily increment. The report can also be viewed from the warehouse manager's role-centered page.

2.8 Additional Case Studies

Case 2.5: Transfers Between Adjacent Warehouses The warehouse manager at a manufacturing company with two adjacent warehouses (within the same AX site) employed transfer journals for moving inventory between the warehouses. A Transfer Journal was initially created and populated with the items and quantities to be moved. The printed version provided a picking list (and turnaround document) for warehouse workers at the originating warehouse, and they entered the actual results for the "from warehouse" on the journal lines. After the material was received, warehouse workers entered the results for the "to warehouse," and posted the transfer journal.

In this scenario, the transfer journals were created by firming planned transfer orders.   This reflects a site-specific policy to "use transfer journals for movements within the site," since both warehouses are within the same AX site. It also reflects the item's coverage policies about the warehouse source for planned transfer orders. Firming will still create actual transfer orders between warehouses in different AX sites.

2.9 Executive Summary

Several fundamentals of the Basic Inventory approach provide the foundation for explaining business processes in subsequent chapters.   These fundamentals include key setup information such as the definition of warehouse locations and the item-related policies for warehouse management.   They include basic inventory transactions such as transfers, adjustments, and cycle counts. Related topics include calculations of space utilization and cycle counting statistics.

Chapter 3

Purchase Order Receiving

The Basic Inventory approach supports several variations for purchase order receiving. For explanatory purposes, it is easiest to start with a simple yet typical business process, and explain the related life cycles, reversing transactions, and key constructs. The basic process provides a baseline for explaining variations, such as different approaches to receiving inspection and load planning for purchases. These topics are reflected in the following sections within the chapter:

1. Basic Process for Purchase Order Receiving
2. Additional Steps in the Basic Process
3. Life Cycles Related to the Basic Process
4. Reversing Transactions in the Basic Process
5. Key Constructs for Purchase Order Receiving
6. Major Variations for Purchase Order Receiving
7. Minor Variations
8. Returns to Vendor

Effective procurement practices represent a critical consideration for purchase order receiving. In order to be effective, the purchase orders should reflect up-to-date S&OP game plans and up-to-date delivery dates and quantities. Additional factors include a manageable level of expediting. These considerations will make life easier for warehouse management.

3.1 Basic Process for Purchase Order Receiving

The business process for purchase order receiving can have many variations. The starting point of a simple yet typical process provides a baseline for explaining the variations. The basic process shown in Figure 3.1 consists of several steps performed by a receiving clerk and warehouse worker. The process starts with the need to report purchase order arrival, and ends with completed reporting. This section provides an overview of the basic process and describes each step in more detail.

3.1   Basic Process for Purchase Order Receiving

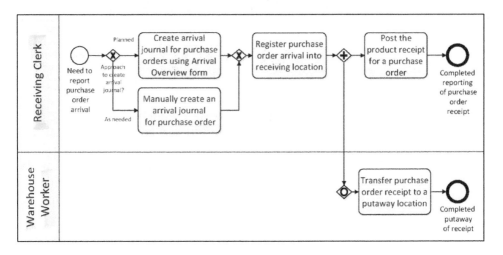

Overview   The receiving clerk typically uses the Arrival Overview form to review a subset of open purchase order line items reflecting user specified criteria, such as the ship-to warehouse, delivery date and delivery mode. The receiving clerk can select purchase order lines, and then create an arrival journal containing the selected lines. Alternatively, the receiving clerk can manually create an Arrival Journal—typically to handle an unplanned receipt. The receiving clerk registers the actual receipts against each journal line item and then posts the journal to update inventory balances. The receiving clerk also identifies the vendor's packing list number when posting the product receipt for the purchase order. For received material with putaway requirements, the warehouse worker uses the Transfer Journal form to report transfers from the receiving location to the putaway location.

Create Arrival Journal for Purchase Orders using the Arrival Overview form   Using the Arrival Overview form, the receiving clerk anticipates arrivals by viewing a subset of open purchase order line items reflecting user specified criteria, such as a ship-to location, delivery date, and delivery mode. The receiving clerk can select purchase order lines and then create an arrival journal containing the selected lines. When selecting purchase order lines, the receiving clerk can optionally analyze the estimated handling time and total weight/volume/pieces.

Manually Create an Arrival Journal for Purchase Orders Using the Arrival Journal form, the receiving clerk can manually create an arrival journal—typically to handle an unplanned receipt.

Register Purchase Order Arrival into Receiving Location The receiving clerk typically prints the line items within an arrival journal as a turnaround document, since it identifies the expected receipts. Using the Arrival Journal form, the receiving clerk enters the vendor's packing list number in the header information, and enters actual receipts for each journal line item (when it differs from expected receipts). The receiving clerk posts the arrival journal after completing the information, which updates inventory balances but not the financial impact.

Post the Product Receipt for a Purchase Order The receiving clerk posts the product receipt for a purchase order, which updates the financial impact of received material. The receiving clerk typically posts the product receipt as a related step on the Arrival Journal form (after posting the arrival journal). In this way, the product receipt reflects the registered information about item arrivals and the previous entry of the vendor's packing list number.

Transfer a Purchase Order Receipt to a Putaway Location When needed, the warehouse worker uses the Transfer Journal form to report a separate putaway transaction after recording purchase order arrival or product receipt into a receiving location. The warehouse worker typically prints the line items within the transfer journal as a turnaround document.

Enforcing the Major Steps in the Basic Process The major steps of registering arrival and posting the product receipt can be enforced by two policies within the Item Model Group assigned to an item. These policies are labeled as the Registration Requirements checkbox and the Receiving Requirements checkbox.

3.2 Additional Steps in the Basic Process

The basic process often includes several additional steps or slight variations. These are not shown in Figure 3.1 so that the diagram does not become too complex. The following steps may be needed.

Alternatives for Posting the Product Receipt The receiving clerk typically posts the product receipt as a related step on the Arrival Journal form (after posting the arrival journal). The Posting Product Receipt form can also be accessed from the Purchase Order form (so that it inherits information from the selected order) or accessed directly (where selection criteria can be used to populate the information). All of these approaches can reflect a quantity basis of *registered* so that the registered information about item arrivals and the previous entry of the vendor's packing list number will be used in posting the product receipt.

Receive Short When No Further Receipts are Expected When posting a product receipt for a purchase order, you can optionally indicate that a purchase order line has been received short (relative to the ordered quantity) and that no further receipts are expected. The status of the purchase order line will be updated to *Received.* Use the *Close for Receipt* checkbox for the relevant line when posting the product receipt.

Requirement for a Complete Delivery (aka Prevent Partial Delivery)
A purchase order can be flagged for complete delivery, which means the entire order quantity must be identified when posting the product receipt. It does not impact the reporting of partial quantities on the arrival journal.

Delay Posting of the Arrival Journal in Order to Indicate Putaway Locations In some scenarios, the receiving clerk enters actual quantities on the arrival journal line items, and then warehouse workers enter the actual putaway locations and post the arrival journal.

Perform Posting of Product Receipt by an Accounts Payable Clerk
In some scenarios, the accounts payable clerk performs posting of product receipts. One rationale is that posting should be tightly controlled because it updates the financial information about receipts. A second rationale is that the quality order results can be considered in the quantity being posted. The clerk can still start from the Arrival Journal form in order to perform posting of the product receipt.

Identify Potential Problems in Delivery Dates The delivery date for a purchase order line provides the basis for expected receiving in the warehouse. In particular, the confirmed delivery date for a purchase line (or a line within a delivery schedule) typically indicates the most realistic, up-to-date information from the vendor. Several standard inquiries identify potential problems about deliveries. You can identify purchase order lines without confirmed delivery dates or with past due delivery dates. You can also identify purchase-related backorders. These problems typically require action by the purchasing agent and coordination with the vendor, but they are also relevant for expected receiving activities in the warehouse.

Identify Purchase-Related Backorders   A purchase-related backorder within AX simply refers to any purchase line with a delivery date prior to a specified date (aka the backorder date). [1] This simple definition includes purchase lines with a partially delivered quantity, where the line has not been closed short when posting the product receipt. A partially delivered quantity is the normal interpretation of a purchase backorder. Standardized inquiries can be used to identify all purchase-related backorders or just those related to a vendor. The purchasing agent typically reviews purchase-related backorders and takes action for a selected backorder. The actions include expediting delivery from the vendor, updating the confirmed delivery date, and/or reducing the quantity for the purchase line.

3.3 Life Cycles Related to the Basic Process

The basic process involves several related constructs where the status for each construct reflects various steps in the process. Figure 3.2 summarizes this information, and identifies those steps representing the essential touch points for updating status. Shading highlights the key constructs of an arrival journal and a transfer journal.

3.4 Reversing Transactions in the Basic Process

The ability to reverse transactions requires an understanding of the current point within the business process and the associated status of key constructs. Borrowing from the previous figure, Figure 3.3 illustrates the steps within the basic process (shown in grey text) and the various points at which you can perform reversing transactions (shown in black text). As identified by step numbers in the figure, you can reverse transactions (3X) after posting the product receipt but prior to entering the vendor's invoice.

---

[1] This simple definition is critical for understanding "backordered lines" with a future delivery date when compared to a specified backorder date in the future.

Figure 3.2   Life Cycles Related to the Basic Process for Purchase Order Receiving

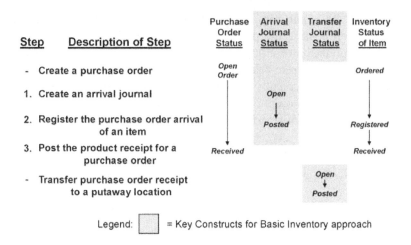

Step	Description of Step	Purchase Order Status	Arrival Journal Status	Transfer Journal Status	Inventory Status of Item
-	Create a purchase order	Open Order			Ordered
1.	Create an arrival journal		Open		
2.	Register the purchase order arrival of an item		Posted		Registered
3.	Post the product receipt for a purchase order	Received			Received
-	Transfer purchase order receipt to a putaway location			Open ↓ Posted	

Legend: ☐ = Key Constructs for Basic Inventory approach

Figure 3.3   Reversing Transactions in the Basic Process for Purchase Order Receiving

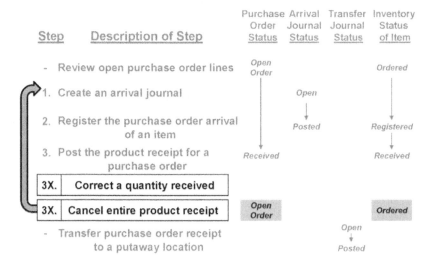

Step	Description of Step	Purchase Order Status	Arrival Journal Status	Transfer Journal Status	Inventory Status of Item
-	Review open purchase order lines	Open Order			Ordered
1.	Create an arrival journal		Open		
2.	Register the purchase order arrival of an item		Posted		Registered
3.	Post the product receipt for a purchase order	Received			Received
3X.	Correct a quantity received				
3X.	Cancel entire product receipt	Open Order			Ordered
-	Transfer purchase order receipt to a putaway location			Open ↓ Posted	

Step 3X: Correct a Quantity Received You can correct a quantity received by starting from the Product Receipt Journal form and selecting the Correct function to access the Product Receipt Correction form. You enter a different received quantity for one or more lines, and the quantity difference (with the previously entered quantity) will be reversed. You can optionally select a reason code for the correction, where codes must be defined on the Vendor Reasons form.

An additional version of a product receipt journal will be automatically created after making a correction. As part of viewing the correction history for a product receipt journal, you can view a comparison of two selected versions in order to identify the new and old values.

Step 3X: Cancel Entire Product Receipt to Reverse the Inventory Transactions You can reverse all transactions related to a product receipt (aka the vendor's packing list number) by starting from the Product Receipt Journal form and selecting the Cancel function. This will remove the items from inventory and reverse the financial impact. Figure 3.3 illustrates the impact on status of cancelling a product receipt, and the arrow indicates the resulting point in the business process. For example, you can start over with registering arrival.

3.5 Key Constructs for Purchase Order Receiving

The basic process for purchase order receiving employs an arrival journal to register receipts for updating inventory balances, and posting of the product receipt for updating the related financial transactions. The posting automatically creates a product receipt journal for viewing the financial impacts. The basic process may also employ transfer journals for putaway purposes. This section summarizes the significance of each of these constructs.

Significance of the Arrival Journal for Purchase Order Receipts An arrival journal provides the basis for identifying expected receipts and also for reporting actual receipt quantities and locations as well as batch and serial numbers if applicable. This is termed "registering the information" (or registration for short) in AX terminology.

Each arrival journal has a system-assigned identifier, and consists of header information and line items. Each line identifies the related purchase order, item and quantity to be received. You enter details about the actual receipt for each line and then post the arrival journal to update inventory balances. However, an additional step is required to update the financial information about received material.

An arrival journal and its line items typically represent the contents of a vendor's packing list, and this packing list number can be identified in the header information for an arrival journal. In this way, after posting the Arrival Journal to update inventory balances, you can easily perform the additional step to post the product receipt (and identify its related packing list number) to update the purchase order.

Significance of Posting the Product Receipt The posting of a product receipt represents the completion of the purchase order receiving process and serves several purposes. As a primary purpose, it updates the financial information about received material and automatically generates the related journal (called the Product Receipt Journal). The financial impact includes purchase price variances for standard cost items. It also updates the purchase order—such as updating the status to *received*—and provides the basis for three-way matching when entering a vendor's invoice.

As part of posting the product receipt, you identify the vendor's packing list number (aka the product receipt number); a companywide policy determines how to handle duplicate numbers.[2] You can also indicate when a purchase order line with a short receipt should be closed, indicating that no further receipts are expected. The quantity basis for posting the product receipt typically reflects the previously registered information about arrivals.

You can access the Posting Product Receipt form for a selected arrival journal or purchase order. It can also be accessed directly where you employ selection criteria for identifying one or more purchase orders.

Significance of the Product Receipt Journal A Product Receipt Journal is automatically created by posting a product receipt. Its identifier reflects the user-assigned product receipt number (aka vendor's packing list number), and consists of a header and line item information. From the header, you can view the related vouchers, distributions, and subledger journal entries. You can also perform reversing transactions for receipts (such as a correction or cancellation). For a selected journal, you can view its line items about the related item, quantity, and purchase order. You can access the Product Receipt Journal form directly or from a selected purchase order.

---

[2] The companywide policy (defined in the Procurement and Sourcing Parameters form) determines whether entry of a duplicate number results in a warning or rejection in order to avoid duplication of reported receipts. Alternatively, you can choose to accept entries of a duplicate number without any warning to the user.

Significance of a Transfer Journal for Purchase Order Putaway A purchase order can be received into a bin location that represents a receiving area, which typically requires an additional step to put away the inventory. A transfer journal can be used to support a separate putaway transaction.

An alternative approach to putaway transactions is supported when using a quarantine order as part of receiving inspection so that it generates a separate putaway transaction for usable material. A subsequent chapter about quality management provides further explanation of quarantine orders (Section 8.3).

Key Forms for Purchase Order Receiving Several key forms correspond to the key constructs, and a quick summary of these key forms is provided below.

◆ *Arrival Journal.* Use this form to identify the expected receipts for a purchase order and to report actual receipts for updating inventory balances. You can register the actual quantity and (when applicable) the location, batch number, and/or serial numbers for the received material.

◆ *Posting Product Receipt.* Use this form to complete the receiving process for a purchase order and update the financial information about received material. Actual posting will automatically create a Product Receipt Journal.

Prior to posting, you must identify the vendor's packing list number (aka product receipt number) which acts as the identifier for the Product Receipt Journal.

◆ *Product Receipt Journal.* Use this form to review the actual receipts related to a vendor's packing list number (aka the product receipt number), and view the vouchers and subledger entries for a selected journal. You can optionally correct or cancel a product receipt.

◆ *Arrival Overview.* Use this form to anticipate receiving activities and generate an arrival journal for selected purchase order lines.

3.6 Major Variations for Purchase Order Receiving

The basic process for production order picking provides the foundation for explaining major variations. The major variations include a simple inventory transaction, the use of receiving inspection and purchase order returns, and the receipts for serialized or batch-controlled items.

Simple Inventory Transaction for Reporting Purchase Order Receipts The receiving clerk can bypass the use of an arrival journal by using a simple inventory transaction, where you register the item when posting the product receipt for a purchase order.   You can also identify registration information for a line item on a purchase order prior to posting the product receipt.

Receive Batch-Controlled Items A batch-controlled item involves the assignment of batch numbers when reporting purchase order arrival. It may also involve reporting of vendor batch information and/or a batch disposition code.

Receive Serialized Items A serialized item involves the assignment of serial numbers when reporting purchase order arrival.

Receiving Inspection for Purchase Order Arrivals There are many variations of receiving inspection for purchased material. For example, the receiving inspection may be performed by receiving clerks at the time of arrival into a receiving location (Case 3.4), or by a quality control clerk reporting against an automatically-created quality order (Case 8.1). In addition, the test results for a quality order may be reported for a small sample while the material remains in a receiving location, or the received material may be placed in a separate QC area until test results have been reported.

Returns to Vendor Returning material to a vendor typically involves a different type of purchase order (termed a returned order) so that you can identify the vendor's RMA number (Return Material Authorization). It can also be handled via a purchase order line item with a negative quantity. A subsequent section provides further explanation about a typical process for purchase order returns (Section 3.9).

3.7 Minor Variations

Several minor variations apply to the basic process for purchase order receiving and its major variations. These include the use of delivery tolerances, safety margins, notes, and the Receipts List. Other minor variations were identified as part of the additional steps for the basic process, such as receiving short, requirements for a complete delivery, and posting product receipts by accounts payable.

♦ Receiving a Special Order
♦ Impact of a Vendor Hold and Other types of Stop Flags
♦ Impact of Delivery Tolerances on Purchase Order Receiving

◆ Modeling the Required Time for Purchase Order Receiving
◆ Effective Use of Notes for Purchase Order Receiving
◆ Using the Receipts List During Purchase Order Receiving

Receiving a Special Order   The receipt of a special order (linked to a sales order) typically involves placement in a designated location for cross docking, so that it can be picked and shipped without putaway to a stocking location. You can identify this location on the sales line so that it is inherited by the related purchase line and displayed on the arrival journal.

An alternative approach to identifying the need for cross docking only applies to WMS-enabled items, where you can employ an Inventory Status. With this alternative, you can define one status as *Cross-Dock*, assign this status to the sales line, and then the status will be inherited by the related purchase line and displayed on the arrival journal.

Impact of a Vendor Hold and Other Types of Stop Flags   The assignment of a vendor hold for "all" transactions will prevent posting of product receipts and result in a corresponding message. However, it does not prevent registration of purchase order arrivals from the vendor. Other types of stop flags include the following.

◆ *Impact of Stopped Transactions for an Item.* The purchase order transactions for an item can be stopped, either as a companywide or site-specific policy. The stopped flag prevents further transactions for an item's existing purchase orders (including registration of arrivals and posting of product receipts) and results in a corresponding message. A similar stopped flag can be specified for an item's inventory transactions, which also prevents further transactions.

◆ *Impact of a Stopped Flag on a Purchase Order Line.* The assignment of a stopped flag for a purchase order line prevents further transactions (including registration of arrivals and posting of product receipts) until it has been removed and results in a corresponding message.

Impact of Delivery Tolerances on Purchase Order Receiving   When delivery tolerances are acceptable, they determine how much the quantities being received can differ from the ordered quantity. Over- and under-delivery tolerances (related to purchase orders) are expressed as a percentage; the values assigned to an item act as defaults for a purchase order line item. Delivery tolerances of zero percent for a purchase order line mean that the received quantity must equal the ordered quantity. A companywide policy (embedded in the Procurement and Sourcing parameters) determines whether over- and under-deliveries will be acceptable for purchase orders. The delivery tolerances are enforced when posting the packing slip for a purchase order, and the over-delivery tolerance is also enforced when reporting arrivals.

Modeling the Required Time for Receiving/Inspection Activities
Some scenarios have a significant time requirement for receiving and inspection activities related to an item's receipt, such as one (1) or more days. A significant time requirement should be included in the supply chain model so that purchase order delivery dates will correctly reflect the required time. The required time can be identified as the receipt safety margin, where you define the number of days as part of the Coverage Group assigned to the item. It is normally assigned as part of the Item Coverage information for the item.

Effective Use of Notes for Purchase Order Receiving Purposes Notes can be entered for a purchase order header and lines, and included in the standard format for printed purchase orders. These notes can be inherited from the vendor and item respectively. However, the notes specific to receiving instructions are not currently included in standard formats; use of notes will require customized formats.

Using the Receipts List During Purchase Order Receiving A printed version of a Receipts List provides reference information for identifying the expected receipts for line items on a purchase order. For example, the expected receipt information includes the item and quantity for each line item. It represents reference information (rather than a turnaround document) because you cannot record actual receipts against the receipts list.

When posting a receipts list for a purchase order, you can optionally specify additional selection criteria (such as the ship-to warehouse and expected delivery date) so that only the applicable lines will be included. Posting the receipts list will automatically generate a Receipts List Journal, which can be subsequently viewed or used for reprinting the document. You can access the Posting Receipts List form for a selected purchase order. It can also be accessed directly or performed via batch processing, where you employ selection criteria for identifying multiple purchase order lines.

3.8 Returns to Vendor

Returning material to a vendor typically involves a different type of purchase order (termed a returned order), so that you can identify the vendor's RMA number (Return Material Authorization). It can also be handled via a purchase order line item with a negative quantity. When using returned orders, the typical process consists of several steps performed by different roles, as illustrated in

Figure 3.4. The key step for warehouse management purposes consists of sending the material to the vendor.

Figure 3.4   Typical Process for a Purchase Order Return

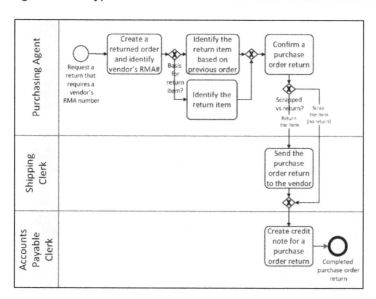

As the starting point for a typical process, the purchasing agent creates a returned order for a specified vendor and identifies the vendor's RMA number. The purchasing agent also creates a line item for each returned item, where the line item identifies an item, a negative quantity, purchase price, ship-from location, and the requested ship date. The line item information can also be created by selecting lines from a previously invoiced purchase order, which helps identify the original purchase price. The purchasing agent confirms a purchase order when information has been completely entered. In some scenarios, these steps are performed by an accounts payable clerk.

The shipping clerk reports the item(s) being sent back for a purchase order return, including the batch number for a batch-controlled item. The shipping clerk uses the Posting Product Receipt form to select a line representing a return, and then identifies the "pick" information about the inventory being returned. The posting can print the packing slip to accompany the items being sent, and it automatically creates a Product Receipt Journal that identifies the financial impact.

3.9 Additional Case Studies

Case 3.1: Correcting Errors about Reported Receipts The receiving clerks at a manufacturing/distribution company would sometimes make a mistake in the reported quantity received. In order to correct the mistake, the supervisor would access the Product Receipt Journal form and select the "Correct" function to access the Product Receipt Correction form. The supervisor would enter the correct quantity for the relevant line and select a reason code for the correction. In this way, the inventory balances and financial information would reflect the correction.

Case 3.2: Modeling the Required Time for Purchase Order Receiving/Inspection A food products manufacturer required test results from an outside service for certain raw materials, which often took five days before the results could be reported for the associated quality order. The five days were included in the receipt safety margin for each item so the material would be scheduled for delivery before the required date. The five days were also reflected in the expected completion date of the quality order so that master scheduling logic recognized the scheduled availability.

Case 3.3: Receiving Inspection with a Separate QC Area For certain purchased items at a manufacturing company, the entire quantity of each purchase order arrival was placed in a separate QC location so that a quality control clerk could report the testing results for the quality order.   After validation, a warehouse worker would report transfers from the QC location to a stocking location. This reflects a different approach than simply reporting test results for a small sample, where the received material stays in a receiving location until validation of the test results.

Case 3.4: Receiving Clerk Assigns Inventory Status during Purchase Order Arrival The warehouse manager and quality manager were considering options for reporting quality problems at the time of purchase order arrival. One approach involved the user-defined values for Inventory Status with possible values of *Good, To-Be-Scrapped, Return-to-Vendor, Needs-Rework,* and *Needs-Inspection*. The default value for Inventory Status was typically identified as *Good* on purchase order lines.

If the receiving clerks noticed a quality problem when reporting purchase order arrival, they would override the Inventory Status to a value of *Needs-Inspection* on the arrival journal. The two managers prepared a diagram of the proposed business process shown in Figure 3.5.

Figure 3.5   Assign Inventory Status during Purchase Order Arrival

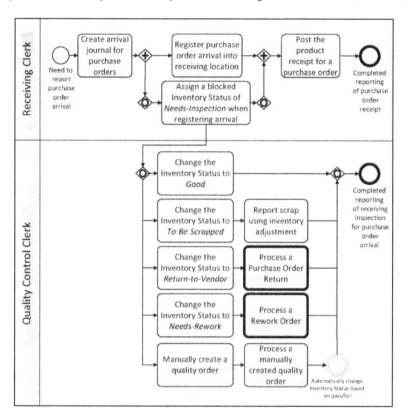

In this example, the receiving clerk identifies material that appears to be damaged or unusable with a blocked status of *Needs-Inspection*, which means it will be listed on the Blocked inventory form to communicate needed follow up by quality management.   The quality control clerk can subsequently make a determination by changing the value of Inventory Status to a value of *Good, To-Be-Scrapped, Return-to-Vendor,* or *Needs-Rework.*   As an additional option, the quality control clerk can manually create and process a quality order.   Other roles were typically responsible for the additional steps of processing a purchase order return or a rework order.

As an alternative, the receiving clerks could be responsible for assigning the other values of the Inventory Status.   However, the quality manager was reluctant to have receiving clerks report anything more than simply assigning a value of *Needs-Inspection*; the manager preferred that a quality control clerk make any further determination.

3.11 Executive Summary

The Basic Inventory approach supports several variations for purchase order receiving. This chapter started with a simple yet typical business process, and explained the related life cycles, reversing transactions, and key constructs. This basic process provided a baseline for explaining variations, such as receiving short, requirements for complete delivery, and different approaches to receiving inspection.

Case studies illustrated some of the variations for purchase order receiving. These included correcting errors about reported receipts, modeling the required time for purchase order receiving/inspection, receiving inspection with a separate QC area, and assigning Inventory Status when reporting purchase order arrival.

Chapter 4

Sales Order Picking/Shipping

The Basic Inventory approach employs an order-based picking list and a related shipment to report sales order fulfillment. For explanatory purposes, it is easiest to start with a simple yet typical business process, and explain the related life cycles, reversing transactions, and key constructs. The basic process provides a baseline for explaining variations, such as the variations of generating picking lists and the use of wave picking. These topics are reflected in the following sections within the chapter:

1. Basic Process for Sales Order Picking/Shipping
2. Additional Steps in the Basic Process
3. Life Cycles Related to the Basic Process
4. Reversing Transactions in the Basic Process
5. Key Constructs for Sales Order Picking/Shipping
6. Major Variations of Sales Order Picking/Shipping
7. Minor Variations
8. Selection Criteria for Generating Picking Lists
9. Generate Picking Lists using the Picking Workbench form
10. Extended Explanation of Related Life Cycles for Picking/Shipping

Realistic delivery promises on sales orders represent a critical consideration for sales order picking/shipping. Delivery promises should reflect S&OP game plans and the delivery dates should reflect up-to-date information. Other factors may apply such as a manageable level of expediting. These considerations will make life easier for warehouse management.

4.1 Basic Process for Sales Order Picking/Shipping

The business process for sales order picking/shipping can have many variations. A simple yet typical process provides a baseline for explaining the variations. The basic process shown in Figure 4.1 consists of several steps performed by a shipping clerk and warehouse worker. The process starts with the need for sales order picking/shipping and ends with completed shipments. This section provides an overview of the basic process and describes each step in more detail.

Figure 4.1   Basic Process for Sales Order Picking/Shipping

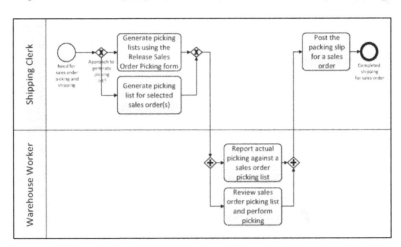

Overview   The shipping clerk typically uses the Release Sales Order Picking form to review and select open sales order lines that require picking/shipping, and then generate the picking lists for selected orders. The generation of a picking list will reserve the item's inventory for the sales line (if not already reserved). The warehouse worker reports actual picking against a sales order picking list, and the shipping clerk reports actual shipment by posting the sales order packing slip for picked items.

Generate Picking Lists Using the Release Sales Order Picking Form
The shipping clerk uses the Release Sales Order Picking form to view a subset of open sales order lines based on selection criteria such as the ship-from warehouse, ship date, mode of delivery and/or customer. The displayed information indicates whether a sales line already has reserved inventory stemming from order entry. When viewing the open sales lines, the shipping clerk can analyze which orders can be picked using available inventory, and then simulate allocation of the inventory to selected sales lines. The selected sales

lines can then be released for picking. This step displays the Posting Picking List form for the selected lines, so that actual posting will generate the picking lists.

Generate Picking List for Selected Sales Order(s) The shipping clerk uses the Posting Picking List form to generate and print the picking list for selected sales order(s), where the query criteria can identify the selected orders. Typical selection criteria include the ship-from warehouse, ship date, mode of delivery and/or customer, and a set of criteria can be predefined with a user-definable name. Alternatively, the customer service rep can generate the picking list as part of order entry for a sales order, where accessing the Posting Picking List form will inherit selection criteria from the sales order.

Review Sales Order Picking List and Perform Picking The warehouse worker can review a printed picking list and perform the picking. The printed picking list identifies the reserved inventory.

Report Actual Picking Against a Sales Order Picking List The warehouse worker uses the Picking List Registration form for reporting actual picking against a picking list and to reduce on hand inventory. In many cases, the shipping clerk simply confirms that the reserved inventory was actually picked. If needed, the shipping clerk can identify the alternative quantity or location that was picked.

Post the Packing Slip for a Sales Order The shipping clerk posts and prints a sales order packing slip (which reflects the picked items) to indicate actual shipment and update the financial information.

Enforcing the Major Steps in the Basic Process The major steps of picking and shipping a sales order can be enforced by two policies within the item model group assigned to an item. These policies are labeled Picking Requirements and Deduction Requirements.

4.2 Additional Steps in the Basic Process

The basic process often involves additional steps or slight variations not shown in Figure 4.1 so that the diagram does not become too complex. The following list and their extended explanations identify some examples. Each topic has been assigned an identifier for ease of reference.

- ◆ A1: Generate/update the Bill of Lading for a sales order shipment
- ◆ A2: Identify and close a sales order line that is shipped short
- ◆ A3: Identify sales orders with partial picking
- ◆ A4: Identify sales order lines picked but not yet shipped

- A5: Identify sales order lines with past due ship dates
- A6: Identify sales-related backorders
- A7: Impact of an Order Hold on sales order picking/shipping
- A8: Review performance metrics for on-time delivery and full quantity

A1: Generate/Update the Bill of Lading for a Sales Order Shipment
Posting the packing slip can also result in automatic generation of a bill of lading, which has a system-assigned identifier. Some information pertaining to the bill of lading is automatically updated, such as the customer, sales order number, delivery address, and the shipped items and quantities. Other information must be manually maintained, including each package type (such as carton), quantity, and weight. Use the Bill of Lading form for data maintenance and document printing. A bill of lading can be manually created to support other types of shipments (such as office furniture) or to support a master bill of lading (such as shipments to a freight forwarder). After creating a bill of lading identifier, for example, you explicitly designate it as a master bill of lading and also assign the identifier to the individual bills of lading associated with it.

A2: Identify and Close a Sales Order Line that is Shipped Short You can indicate that a sales line with a shipped short quantity should be closed when posting the packing slip for the sales order.

A3: Identify Sales Orders with Partial Picking One indicator of needed actions for warehouse management consists of sales orders with partially completed picking. You can identify these needed actions using a standard form (labeled All Partially Picked Orders, within Accounts Receivable). The form identifies any sales order with one or more line items that have a partially picked quantity. It does not include sales orders with a delivered status where a sales line was shipped short and closed.

A4: Identify Sales Order Lines Picked but not yet Shipped One indicator of needed actions for warehouse management consists of sales order line items which have been picked but not yet shipped as of today's date. You can identify these needed actions using a standard report (labeled Inventory Picked not Delivered, within Inventory Management).

A5: Identify Sales Order Lines with Past Due Ship Dates One indicator of needed actions for warehouse management consists of sales order line items with past-due ship dates   You can identify these needed actions using a standard form (labeled Delayed Shipments, within Sales and Marketing), which lists the sales lines with a promised ship date that is past due relative to a specified backorder date.

A6: Identify Sales-Related Backorders   A sales-related backorder within AX simply refers to any sales line with a ship date prior to a specified date (aka the backorder date).[1] This simple definition also applies to a sales line with an unshipped or partially shipped quantity, where the line has not been closed short when reporting actual shipment. This represents the more common interpretation of a sales-related backorder. Some scenarios need to identify the quantity for an unshipped or partially shipped line as "backordered" on sales order documents.[2] A standard inquiry provides information about sales-related backorders (labeled Backorder Lines, within Sales and Marketing).

The customer service rep typically reviews sales-related backorders and takes action for a selected backorder, but the information is also critical for the warehouse manager. The actions include updating the promise date or reducing the quantity for the sales order line, or a request to expedite a supply order.

A7: Impact of an Order Hold on Sales Order Picking/Shipping   The assignment of a Hold Code to a sales order will prevent any picking/shipping transactions until the Hold Code has been cleared. It results in a corresponding warning message when attempting to enter transactions.

A8: Review Performance Metrics for On-Time Delivery and Full Quantity   Two performance metrics include on-time delivery and full quantity delivery, typically measured over a specified time interval.

4.3 Life Cycles Related to the Basic Process

The basic process involves several related constructs, where the status for each construct reflects various steps in the process. Figure 4.2 summarizes this information for the basic process, and only displays those steps representing the essential touch points for updating status. Grey shading highlights the key constructs of a picking list, output order and shipment.

As shown in the figure, the first step will create a picking list (with line items reflecting output orders) and a corresponding shipment. It should be noted that the status for a shipment is identified by the combination of two fields termed the Shipment Status and the Physical Update Status. For example, the combination of *Activated* + *Waiting* indicates the shipment has been created. The right side of

---

[1] This simple definition is critical for understanding "backordered lines" with a future ship date when compared to a specified backorder date in the future.
[2] The treatment of unshipped and partially shipped line items is defined by the Backorder Tracking policy for printing packing slips and invoices (within the Forms Setup form in Accounts Receivable).

the figure shows the inventory status for an item on a sales order line.   For example, various steps in the process will change this status from *on order* to *reserved physical, picked,* and *deducted.*

Figure 4.2   Life Cycles Related to the Basic Process for Sales Order Picking/Shipping

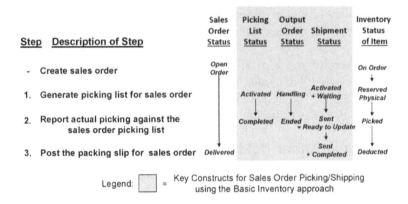

Step	Description of Step	Sales Order Status	Picking List Status	Output Order Status	Shipment Status	Inventory Status of Item
-	Create sales order	Open Order				On Order
1.	Generate picking list for sales order		Activated	Handling	Activated + Waiting	Reserved Physical
2.	Report actual picking against the sales order picking list		Completed	Ended	Sent + Ready to Update	Picked
3.	Post the packing slip for sales order	Delivered			Sent + Completed	Deducted

Legend: ☐ = Key Constructs for Sales Order Picking/Shipping using the Basic Inventory approach

Information about related life cycles provides the foundation for explaining the reversing transactions which is covered in the next section.   An extended explanation of each status is deferred until the end of the chapter (Section 4.10).

4.4 Reversing Transactions in the Basic Process

The ability to reverse transactions requires an understanding of the current point within the business process and the associated status of key constructs. Borrowing from the previous figure, Figure 4.3 illustrates the steps within the basic process (shown in grey text), and the various points at which you can perform reversing transactions (shown in black text).   The figure also illustrates the impact of a reversing transaction on status, and the arrows indicate the resulting point in the business process.   As identified by step numbers in the figure, you can reverse transactions (1X) after initially generating a picking list (2X) after reporting actual picking and (4X) after reporting actual shipment.

Step 1X: Reverse Transaction after Generating Picking List   You can delete an output order (on the Output Order form) prior to actual picking, which automatically deletes the corresponding line on a picking list.   Alternatively, you can cancel a picking list line or the entire picking list, which also deletes the corresponding output order(s).   A deleted output order no longer has a status, as shown by a value of "N/A" within the figure.

Figure 4.3   Reversing Transactions in the Basic Process
for Sales Order Picking/Shipping

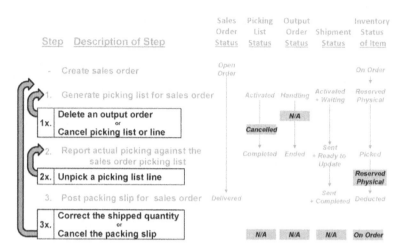

Step 2X: Reverse Transaction after Actual Picking   You can unpick a transaction prior to actual shipment by using the Unpick function on the Picking List Registration form.

Step 3X: Correct the Shipped Quantity or Cancel the Packing Slip Information can be corrected or cancelled after posting the sales order packing slip but before you generate the invoice.   You perform the correction or cancellation from the Packing Slip Journal form, as described below.

◆ *Correct the quantity for a packing slip.*   When you select the Correct function, you access the Correct Packing Slip form in order to enter a different shipped quantity.   The quantity difference (with the previously entered quantity) will be reversed.

◆ *Cancel a packing slip.*   When you select the Cancel function, you will cancel the sales order packing slip.

4.5 Key Constructs for Sales Order Picking/Shipping

The Basic Inventory approach for sales order picking/shipping involves several key constructs in addition to the sales order.   These constructs include output orders, picking lists, and shipment.   An output order represents a request for picking a sales order line item, and provides the basis for line items on a picking list.   A picking list indicates what needs to be picked, and the printed picking list serves as a turnaround document for warehouse workers.   You report actual picking against the picking list.

Significance of an Output Order for Sales Order Picking   An output order (also termed an Inventory Order) represents a request for picking a sales order line item. Each output order has a system-assigned number and identifies the source information such as the sales order, item, quantity, ship-from warehouse, and ship date. When generating a picking list for a sales order, the system automatically creates an output order for each applicable line item and assigns it to the picking list. You can subsequently view the output orders that have been assigned to a picking list. Actual picking will automatically update the output order status from the initial value of *handling* to *ended,* and you can view the inventory transactions associated with the output order.

An output order can be deleted from a picking list prior to actual picking. Deletion of all output orders assigned to a picking list will also delete the picking list itself. Generating another picking list for the sales order will automatically create the output orders.

After generating a sales order picking list, and making changes to the sales order such as a quantity increase or an additional line, you can generate an additional picking list that will also automatically create output orders for the related changes.

Significance of the Picking List for a Sales Order   A picking list indicates what needs to be picked, and the printed picking list serves as a turnaround document for warehouse workers. You report actual picking against the picking list. A sales order will have a single picking list in a simple scenario, such as a sales order with a single ship-from warehouse, one delivery mode, and a single ship date.

Each sales order picking list has a system-assigned identifier (also termed the picking route number), and one or more line items reflect the assignment of output orders to the picking list. A customer service rep can generate the picking list(s) from the Sales Order form in the context of order entry. Alternatively, the warehouse personnel can use other approaches to subsequently generate the picking lists based on selection criteria.   In either case, the generation of a picking list reserves inventory for each sales order line (if not already reserved), and the printed picking list identifies the reserved material. Several options can be used to print or e-mail the picking list. After generating a picking list, it can be viewed on the Picking List Journal form and optionally reprinted.

Separate picking lists will be generated for a sales order when the sales lines identify more than one ship-from site or mode of delivery.[3] Separate picking lists may also reflect the selection criteria within the approach for generating picking lists, such as selection criteria about different ship dates or expedite codes on sales lines.

Significance of a Shipment for a Sales Order Each sales order picking list has a related shipment which the system automatically creates when you generate a picking lists. Each shipment has a system-assigned identifier. A shipment has no particular significance for the Basic Inventory approach. As a confusing factor, the Advanced WMS approach employs a different construct with the same name.

Significance of the Packing Slip for a Sales Order You post a sales order packing slip to indicate actual shipment of the picked items and to update the financial information. You can also print the packing slip.

Posting a sales order packing slip creates a packing slip journal, which can be viewed on the Packing Slip Journal form. Each journal has a system-assigned number. When viewing a selected packing slip journal, you can print the related packing slip, review additional information (such as related voucher transactions), and send an electronic version of the Advanced Ship Notice (ASN) to the customer. You can also correct a transaction quantity or cancel the related shipment transactions, but only before the related invoice has been posted.

Key Forms for Sales Order Picking/Shipping Several key forms correspond to the key constructs, and a quick summary of these key forms is provided below.

◆ *Posting Picking List.* Use this form to generate and print picking lists for selected sales order line items. Actual posting will automatically create a Picking List Journal.

◆ *Picking List Journal.* Use this form to review sales order picking lists as well as access the Picking List Registration form for a selected picking list.

◆ *Picking List Registration.* Use this form to report actual picking against a sales order picking list.

◆ *Posting Packing Slip.* Use this form to post the packing slip for selected sales orders. Actual posting will automatically create a Packing Slip Journal.

---

[3] A companywide policy (within the Accounts Receivable Parameters) determines whether separate picking lists will be generated for different delivery modes on sales lines within a sales order.

◆ *Packing Slip Journal.* Use this form to review sales order packing lists and related information about vouchers and subledger entries. You can also make corrections to a selected packing slip or cancel it.

◆ *Release Sales Order Picking.* Use this form to review a subset of sales order line items based on selection criteria. When you release selected lines for picking, you automatically access the Posting Picking List form to generate and print the picking lists.

4.6 Major Variations of Sales Order Picking/Shipping

The basic process for sales order picking/shipping provides the baseline for explaining variations. These variations include a simple inventory transaction—the picking of serialized or batch-controlled items, the selection criteria for generating picking lists, and use of the Picking Workbench for wave picking purposes. One of the variations in the basic process—for using the Release Sales Order Picking form—is repeated here for completeness sake.

Simple Inventory Transaction for Sales Order Picking/Shipping The shipping clerk can bypass the use of picking lists and shipments by using a simple inventory transaction, where you report actual picking when posting the packing slip for a sales order. This simple inventory transaction applies to both the Basic Inventory Approach and the Advanced WMS approach.

Picking Batch-Controlled Items The sales order picking list can identify the reserved material for the specific batch(es) to be picked. With shelf-life items and FEFO reservation logic, for example, the reserved material reflects the inventory's expiration date and the customer requirements for remaining shelf life. Alternatively, the reserved material can reflect a batch reservation during sales order entry based on the customer's requirements for batch attributes.

Picking Serialized Items The serial number(s) can be identified when reporting actual picking against the sales order picking list.

Shipping Serialized Items with Deferred Assignment of Serial Numbers With the deferred approach, you register the item's serial number(s) when posting the sales order packing slip by accessing the Serial Numbers form for the line item. The serial numbers are not identified when reporting actual picking against the sales order picking list.

Selection Criteria for Generating Sales Order Picking Lists Different selection criteria can be used to generate sales order picking lists, such as the ship-from warehouse, ship date, customer and/or mode of delivery. Additional criteria include expedite policies that have been assigned to the sales order header and line items, and the customer classification code assigned to customers. A subsequent section provides further explanation of the variations in selection criteria (Section 4.8).

Generate Picking Lists Using the Release Sales Order Picking Form
The shipping clerk uses the Release Sales Order Picking form to view a subset of open sales order lines based on selection criteria, and release selected lines in order to generate picking lists. As one advantage, this form displays related information about the ability to deliver the order and the need for allocation. You can temporarily reserve the inventory for selected lines. It also displays information about other requirements for the item stemming from production or transfers. As a result, it makes it easier to selectively identify which sales lines should be released for picking. As a related advantage, the form supports a stepwise allocation of available inventory based on selection criteria (including the Customer Classification Code about customer priority), thereby avoiding the complexities of automatic allocation approaches.

In terms of shortcomings, the form does not display a sales line when no inventory exists for the item, but this can be corrected via customization. A related shortcoming concerns the lack of visibility about scheduled receipts, which would be helpful when production orders (or other supply orders) will be imminently received.

Generate Picking Lists Using the Picking Workbench Approach
The Picking Workbench provides an alternative approach to the generation of sales order picking lists that reflects the wave picking concept. That is, the picking lists can be grouped together under a separate identifier (termed a picking batch) and assigned to a warehouse worker. In addition, it can suggest the appropriate box size(s) and number of boxes for packing the items when generating the picking lists.

4.7 Minor Variations

Several minor variations apply to the basic process of sales order shipping/shipping and its major variations. Some minor variations were identified as part of the additional steps for the basic process, such as identifying needed actions for warehouse management. The following list and their extended explanations identify some other examples. Each topic has been assigned an identifier for ease of reference.

- ◆ A1: Quality orders for sales order picking/shipping
- ◆ A2: Impact of a customer pickup on picking/shipping
- ◆ A3: Impact of a sales order hold and other types of holds
- ◆ A4: Significance of Ship Complete policies for a sales order
- ◆ A5: Impact of Delivery Tolerances on picking/shipping
- ◆ A6: Significance of Expedite Policies for picking/shipping
- ◆ A7: Modeling the required time for picking/shipping activities
- ◆ A8: Relevance of Order Entry Deadlines for picking/shipping activities
- ◆ A9: Effective Use of Notes for Picking/Shipping Purposes

A1: Quality Orders for Sales Order Picking/Shipping A quality order can be automatically generated when you generate a picking list or post the packing slip for a sales order, as defined by Quality Associations related to sales orders for an item. For example, tests may be required before an item can be actually picked (or shipped), and the associated blocking rules can prevent further transactions (such as actual picking or shipping) until the quality order has been validated. In addition, a warning message is displayed on subsequent transactions when validation fails.

A2: Impact of a Customer Pickup on Picking/Shipping The Sales Pickup form displays sales orders having one or more line items with a delivery mode for customer pickup, and provides a short-cut approach for reporting shipment and invoicing transactions. However, you can also perform the normal picking and shipping steps for a customer pickup.

A3: Impact of a Sales Order Hold and Other Types of Holds The assignment of a Hold Code to a sales order will prevent any picking/shipping transactions until the Hold Code has been cleared. Other types of holds include customer holds and stopped flags.

- ◆ *Impact of a Customer Hold.* The assignment of the hold policy of "all" to a customer will prevent any picking/shipping transactions for the customer.

- ◆ *Impact of Stopped Transactions for an Item.* The sales order transactions for an item can be stopped, either as a companywide or site-specific policy within the item's default order policies. The stopped flag prevents further transactions for an item's existing sales orders, including picking/shipping transactions. A similar stopped flag can be specified for an item's inventory transactions, which also prevents further transactions.

A4: Significance of Ship Complete (aka Prevent Partial Delivery) Policies for a Sales Order A sales order line can be flagged as "Ship Complete", which is termed the "Prevent Partial Delivery" policy when using the new Dynamics AX. The policy means that you will receive an error unless you ship the entire quantity when posting the sales order packing slip. An additional "ship complete" flag for the entire sales order has a slightly different significance as it prevents the generation of a sales order picking list until all lines have sufficient inventory to be reserved for the ordered quantity. Hence, using both policies will help ensure that all lines will be picked, and that order quantities for individual lines will be shipped complete.

As an alternative approach, the concept of "ship complete" can be enforced using the delivery tolerance functionality, since delivery tolerances of zero percent for a sales line mean that the shipped quantity must equal the ordered quantity. It is also possible to enforce a companywide policy so that any over- and under-delivery quantities are not acceptable.   The next point provides further explanation of delivery tolerances.

A5: Impact of Delivery Tolerances on Picking/Shipping When delivery tolerances are acceptable, they determine how much the quantities being picked and shipped for a sales line can differ from the ordered quantity. Over- and under-delivery tolerances (related to sales orders) are expressed as a percentage; the values assigned to an item act as defaults for a sales order line item. Delivery tolerances of zero percent for a sales line mean that the shipped quantity must equal the ordered quantity. A companywide policy (embedded in the A/R parameters) determines whether over- and under-deliveries will be acceptable for sales orders.

An over-delivery tolerance applies to both the picked quantity and the shipped quantity for a sales line. For example, the system displays an error message and prevents over-picking (beyond the over-delivery tolerance) when reporting the quantity picked, as well as over-shipping (beyond the delivery tolerance) when posting the sales order packing slip.

An under-delivery tolerance only applies to the shipped quantity for a sales line. For example, you cannot post the packing slip for an under-shipped quantity (beyond the under-delivery tolerance) in conjunction with the "close short" flag—the system displays an error message.

A6: Significance of Expedite Policies on Picking/Shipping Expedite policies can be assigned to a sales order header and line items, and they provide selection criteria for generating sales order picking lists. They do not directly impact picking/shipping activities, and they are sometimes included in printed picking lists as reference information. A subsequent section provides further explanation of expedite codes in the context of generating picking lists (Section 4.8).

A7: Modeling the Required Time for Picking/Shipping Activities

Some scenarios have a significant time requirement for picking/shipping activities related to a sales order (such as 1 or 2 days), while many others have a much shorter preparation time. A significant time requirement should be included in the supply chain model so that (1) promised ship dates will reflect the required time and (2) picking will be scheduled prior to the ship date.

◆ *Identify the Required Time for Picking/Shipping as a Safety Margin for a Salable Item.* The required time can be identified as the issue safety margin for a salable item, where you define the number of days as part of the Coverage Group assigned to the item. For example, when demands exist for an item with one day prep time, master scheduling logic will generate planned orders to arrive one day before the demand date. As another consideration, when using the Release Sales Order Picking form to anticipate picking activities, you should release orders for picking one day prior to the ship date.

◆ *Include Required Time for Picking/Shipping in Delivery Promises* The required time (expressed as the issue safety margin described above) can be included in delivery promises based on ATP logic, where you assign a delivery date control policy of "ATP plus issue margin" to the saleable item as part of its default order policies. For example, when entering a sales line for a stocked item with one day prep time, the earliest possible promised date will be one day later.

Some scenarios do not use ATP logic as the basis for delivery promises, such as using CTP logic for make-to-order items. In many of these scenarios, the required time can be modeled by the sales lead time assigned to an item as part of its default order policies.

A8: Relevance of Order Entry Deadlines for Picking/Shipping Activities

Some scenarios involve same day shipments for sales orders that have been entered by a specified deadline. This order entry deadline frequently represents a prerequisite for meeting the departure time of a shipping vehicle so that adequate time is available for picking/shipping activities. An order entry deadline also means that an order entered after the specified time will be treated as if it were entered the next day, thereby affecting the assignment of a promised ship date. You define a set of deadlines for each day within a week (termed an order entry deadline group), and then assign the deadline group to each customer and site.

A9: Effective Use of Notes for Picking/Shipping Purposes The printed version of a picking list and packing list can optionally include notes about the sales order header and/or line items that can guide picking/shipping activities. It is often helpful to create a user-defined note type that is only applicable to picking/shipping instructions so that notes can be entered (and printed) for just the applicable note type.

4.8 Selection Criteria for Generating Sales Order Picking Lists

Several approaches can be used to generate picking lists based on selection criteria. Example selection criteria are summarized in Figure 4.4 and described below. The figure indicates the applicable constructs for each selection criteria, such as the sales order line or header. It also highlights several selection criteria (via light grey shading) which provide the basis for prioritizing picking/shipping activities, such as the ship date and expedite code for a sales line.

Figure 4.4   Example Selection Criteria for
Generating Sales Order Picking Lists

Field Name	Applicable Construct		
	SO Line	SO Header	Customer
Ship from site/warehouse	Yes	Yes	N/A
Ship date	Yes	Yes	N/A
Mode of delivery	Yes	Yes	N/A
Expedite code	Yes	Yes	N/A
Expedited shipment flag	N/A	Yes	N/A
Sales order priority for fulfillment	N/A	Yes	N/A
Customer classification group	N/A	N/A	Yes
Customer		Yes	N/A
Ship-to address information	Yes	Yes	N/A
Shipping carrier/service	Yes	Yes	N/A

Basis for Prioritizing Picking and Shipping

◆ *Ship-From Site and Warehouse.* The ship-from site and warehouse provide an organizing focus for picking/shipping activities.

◆ *Ship Date.* The ship date provides the primary basis for scheduling and prioritizing the picking/shipping activities, and is frequently used in conjunction with other prioritization criteria. The confirmed ship date is typically used, although the requested ship date may be used in some cases.

♦ *Mode of Delivery.* The mode of delivery provides another organizing focus for picking/shipping activities, especially when preparing shipments for a scheduled pickup time. A sales order may have multiple picking lists that reflect different delivery modes on sales lines. A delivery mode may reflect faster or expedited delivery, and can be associated with an Expedite code.

♦ *Expedite Code.* A user-defined Expedite code can be assigned to a sales order header and/or line item to indicate the need for expediting. In addition, you can associate an Expedite code with a mode of delivery so that selecting the expedited mode of delivery also updates the Expedite code on a sales order.

♦ *Expedited Shipment Flag.* The expedite shipment flag can only be assigned to a sales order header, and it provides an additional basis for expediting. As the primary purpose, it works in conjunction with the shipping carrier assigned to a sales order in order to include the carrier's shipping charges (for expedited shipment) when they are normally considered as free for orders exceeding a specified total amount.

♦ *Sales Order Priority for Fulfillment.* A predefined priority can only be assigned to a sales order header, and it provides an additional basis for expediting. The ten predefined values reflect different priorities, ranging from High (1) to Low(10).

♦ *Customer Classification Group.* A user-defined customer classification group can be assigned to a customer, and provides one approach to prioritize the generation of picking lists when using the Release Sales Order Picking form.

♦ *Customer.* A selected customer provides another organizing focus for picking/shipping activities, such as generating picking lists for shipping sales orders to a customer.

♦ *Ship-To Address Information.* Various elements of the address can be used as an organizing focus of picking/shipping activities, such as generating picking lists for shipping sales orders to the same address.

♦ *Shipping Carrier and Carrier Service.* The shipping carrier and carrier service can be used as an organizing focus of picking/shipping activities, especially when preparing shipments for a scheduled pickup time by the carrier.

4.9 Generate Picking Lists Using the Picking Workbench Form

The Picking Workbench provides an alternative approach to the generation of sales order picking lists that reflects the wave picking concept. That is, the picking lists can be grouped together under a separate identifier (termed a picking batch) and assigned to a warehouse worker. It optionally provides boxing logic to suggest the appropriate box size(s) and number of boxes for packing the items. Further explanation is provided in the complete book about warehouse management.

4.10 Extended Explanation of Related Life Cycles for Picking/Shipping

The basic process for sales order picking/shipping involves several related constructs of picking lists, output orders and shipments, with a status automatically updated by steps in the process. The life cycles were previously illustrated for the basic process (Figure 4.2). The same constructs and life cycles are also employed in transfer order picking/shipping (Figure 5.2). This section provides an extended explanation of the status for each construct, and it applies to both sales orders and transfer orders.

Status of a Picking List A status applies to a picking list and each line item. The status for a picking list indicates the following steps in its life cycle:

◆ *Activated.* The status indicates the picking list has been created. The picking list can be cancelled.

◆ *Started.* The status indicates that one line item has been picked when the picking list contains multiple lines. Alternatively, the status reflects a manual update to indicate that picking has started.

◆ *Completed.* The status indicates all line items have been picked for the picking list.

◆ *Cancelled.* The status indicates the picking list has been cancelled, or that all line items have been cancelled.

Status of a Line Item on a Picking List   The status for a line item on a sales order picking list indicates the following steps in its life cycle.

◆ *Activated.* The status indicates the line item has been created. The line item can be deleted or cancelled if needed for reversing transactions.

◆ *Picked.* The status indicates the line item has been picked. The line item can be unpicked if needed for reversing transactions.

◆ *Completed.* The status indicates the line item has been picked for the picking list.

◆ *Cancelled.* The status indicates the line item has been cancelled.

Status of an Output Order   The status for an output order indicates the following steps in its life cycle.

◆ *Handling.* The status indicates the output order has been created for a line item on an order, and assigned to a picking list line item. It also applies to an output order for a picking list line item that has been partially picked.

◆ *Ended.* The status indicates the related picking list line item has been completely picked. It can also indicate the related picking list line item has been cancelled.

Status of a Shipment   The status for a shipment is identified by the combination of two fields—termed the Shipment Status and the Physical Update Status—which indicate the following steps in its life cycle. For example, the combination of *Activated + Waiting* indicates the shipment has been created.

◆ *Activated + Waiting.* The status indicates the shipment has been created, along with its associated picking list.

◆ *Sent + Ready for Update.* The status indicates the associated picking list has been completely picked.

◆ *Sent + Completed.* The status indicates the associated order has been shipped.

◆ *Cancelled.* The status indicates the associated picking list has been cancelled.

4.11 Additional Case Studies

Case 4.1: Sales Order Shipments from a Remote Warehouse Several remote warehouses for a distribution operation did not have on-line access for reporting AX transactions. In order to communicate the need for sales order shipments from the remote warehouses, the DRP coordinator generated the sales order picking lists and e-mailed a copy to the relevant contact person. The contact person sent a return e-mail after completing the requested shipments, and the DRP coordinator simply posted each completed picking list and the related sales order packing slip.

Case 4.2: Expedite Policies for Sales Order Picking The customer service reps at a manufacturing/distribution company used several different approaches to indicate the need for expediting when the rep was entering a sales order or its line items. As the starting point, the assignment of shipment and delivery dates reflected available to promise logic so that unrealistic dates could not be assigned. The customer service reps could then assign an expedited mode of delivery which also resulted in the automatic assignment of a expedite code. The shipping clerks would use this expedite code (and mode of delivery) to help prioritize the generation of sales order picking lists and ultimately provide expedited service.

Case 4.3: Correcting Errors about a Reported Shipment The warehouse workers and shipping clerks at a manufacturing/distribution company would sometimes make a mistake in the reported quantity shipped. In order to correct the mistake, the supervisor would access the Packing Slip Journal form and select the "Correct" function to access the Correct Packing Slip form. In this way, the inventory balances and financial information would reflect the correction.

Case 4.4: Print an MSDS Document to Accompany a Sales Order Shipment A manufacturing company produced several items that required an MSDS (Material Safety Data Sheet) document. This had several impacts. For example, when entering a sales order line for an item designated as hazardous material, a warning message can be displayed about sending the latest active MSDS document to the customer. This warning message occurs when the customer has not yet received the item's MSDS document, or when a newer version (defined by the document's effective date) needs to be sent. At the time of shipping, the shipping clerk would print the relevant MSDS documents when posting the packing list for the sales order. This transaction was prevented when a document's expiry date has been exceeded.

4.12 Executive Summary

The Basic Inventory approach employs an order-based picking list and a related shipment to report sales order fulfillment. This chapter started with a simple yet typical business process, and explained the related life cycles, reversing transactions, and key constructs. The basic process provided a baseline for explaining variations, such as the variations of generating picking lists.

Several case studies illustrated variations for sales order picking/shipping. These included sales order shipments from a remote warehouse, expedite policies for sales order picking, and correcting errors about a reported shipment.

Chapter 5

Transfer Order
Picking/Shipping

The Basic Inventory approach employs an order-based picking list and a related shipment to report transfer order fulfillment. As an explanatory approach, it is easiest to start with a simple yet typical business process, and explain the related life cycles, transactions, and key constructs. The basic process provides a baseline for explaining variations, such as different ways to generate picking lists and the use of wave picking. These topics are reflected in the following sections within the chapter:

1. Basic Process for Transfer Order Picking/Shipping
2. Additional Steps in the Basic Process
3. Life Cycles Related to the Basic Process
4. Reversing Transactions in the Basic Process
5. Key Constructs for Transfer Order Picking/Shipping
6. Major Variations of Transfer Order Picking/Shipping
7. Minor Variations

Effective distribution planning represents a critical consideration for transfer order picking/shipping and receiving. In order to be effective, the requirements for transfer orders should reflect S&OP game plans, a reasonable model of the supply chain, and other factors such as a manageable level of expediting. These considerations will make life easier for warehouse management.

The AX functionality for picking/shipping a transfer order shares a high degree of similarity with the functionality for sales orders, but there are several differences. These differences include the approach for reporting actual shipment and the ability to reverse shipment transactions. In addition, the use of order holds, expedite codes, and quality orders do not apply to transfer orders. Hence, this chapter provides a completely separate explanation about transfer orders, even though a few topics must be repeated for completeness sake.

59

5.1 Basic Process for Transfer Order Picking/Shipping

The business process for transfer order picking/shipping can have many variations. A simple yet typical process provides a baseline for explaining the variations. The basic process shown in Figure 5.1 consists of several steps typically performed by a shipping clerk and a warehouse worker. The process starts with the need for transfer order picking/shipping and ends with completed shipments. This section provides an overview of the basic process and describes each step in more detail.

Figure 5.1   Basic Process for Transfer Order Picking/Shipping

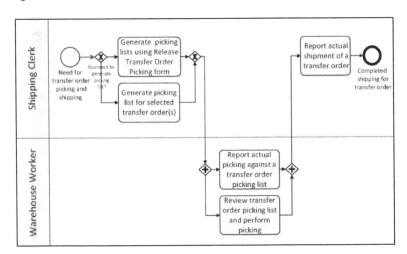

Overview   The shipping clerk typically uses the Release Transfer Order Picking form to review and select open transfer order lines that require picking/shipping, and then generate the picking lists for selected orders. The generation of a picking list will reserve the item's inventory (if not already reserved). The warehouse worker reports actual picking against a transfer order picking list, and the shipping clerk reports actual shipment of the transfer order.

Generate Picking Lists Using the Release Transfer Order Picking Form   The shipping clerk uses the Release Transfer Order Picking form to view a subset of open transfer order lines based on selection criteria. The displayed information indicates whether a transfer line already has reserved inventory. The shipping clerk can analyze which lines can be picked using available inventory, and then simulate allocation of the inventory to selected transfer lines. The selected transfer lines can then be released for picking, which displays the

Posting Picking List form for the selected lines so that actual posting will generate the picking lists. Generation of a picking list will reserve the item's inventory for each transfer line (if not already reserved).

Generate Picking List for Selected Transfer Order(s)   The shipping clerk generates and prints the picking list for selected transfer orders by using the Posting Picking List form. It can be accessed from the Transfer Order form for a selected order, although it is commonly accessed directly in order to generate picking lists for multiple orders based on selection criteria. Typical selection criteria include the ship-from warehouse, ship date, and mode of delivery. Different sets of selection criteria are commonly predefined with a user-definable name in order to model typical variations in the business process. Generation of a picking list will reserve the item's inventory for each transfer line (if not already reserved).

Review Transfer Order Picking List and Perform Picking   The warehouse worker can review a printed picking list and perform the picking. The printed picking list identifies the reserved inventory.

Report Actual Picking Against a Transfer Order Picking List   The warehouse worker reports actual picking against a picking list using the Picking List Registration form. It can be accessed from the Transfer Order form for a selected order, although it is commonly accessed directly in order to report actual picking for one or more transfer orders based on selection criteria. Typical selection criteria include the transfer order number, ship-from warehouse, ship date, and/or mode of delivery. In many cases, the shipping clerk simply confirms that the reserved inventory was actually picked. If needed, the shipping clerk can identify the alternative quantity or location that was picked, or close a line item when reporting less than the ordered quantity.

Report Actual Shipment of a Transfer Order   The shipping clerk reports actual shipment of a transfer order using the Shipment [for Transfer Orders] form. It can be accessed from the Transfer Order form for a selected order, although it is commonly accessed directly in order to report actual picking for one or more transfer orders based on selection criteria. Typical selection criteria include the transfer order number, ship-from warehouse, ship date, and/or mode of delivery. The shipping clerk typically employs the actual picking information as the basis for actual shipment, and can optionally specify a tracking ID for the shipment.

Enforcing the Major Steps in the Typical Business Process   The major step of picking a transfer order can be enforced by the Picking Requirement policy within the Item Model Group assigned to an item.

5.2 Additional Steps in the Basic Process

The basic process typically includes several additional steps not shown in Figure 5.1 so that the diagram does not become too complex. Examples include the following steps.

Ship Short When No Further Shipments are Expected When using the Shipment form to report actual shipment of a transfer order line, you can optionally indicate that a line has been shipped short (relative to the order quantity) and that no further shipments are expected. Use the *Close* checkbox for the relevant line, and this will also update its status to *Shipped.*

Assign a Tracking ID to a Transfer Order Shipment You can optionally assign a Tracking ID when reporting actual shipment using the Shipment form. The Tracking ID only provides reference information.

Identify Transfer Order Lines Picked but not yet Shipped One indicator of needed actions for warehouse management consists of transfer order line items which have been picked but not yet shipped as of today's date. You can identify these needed actions using a standard report labeled Inventory Picked not Delivered.

Print Shipment Documents for Transfer Orders You can print a Transfer Order Shipment from the Transfer Order form, or by using the Transfer Order Shipment report and its associated dialogue about selection criteria. The document identifies the transfer order number and related information, such as the ship-to address, mode of delivery, posting date, and tracking number (if specified), as well as information about its line items.

Review In Transit Inventory for an Item You can view an item's in-transit inventory on various on-hand inquiries, or view the on-hand inquiries for the in-transit warehouse and its location.

Review Transfer Order History The Transfer Order History form displays all transfer orders with separate lines for the related shipment and receipt transactions, and the related line items for a selected transaction. It displays the posting date and voucher for each transaction line, and the tracking ID (if specified) for a shipment transaction.

Review the Transfer Overview Report This report provides a one line summary of each transfer order, including its status, the ship-from and ship-to warehouses, and the ship and receipt dates. It also identifies the item and quantity for each line item on a transfer order. You can specify selection criteria as part of the associated report dialogue—such as the relevant ship-from warehouse, ship date and order status—in order to view the desired subset of transfer orders.

5.3 Life Cycles Related to the Basic Process

The basic process for transfer order picking/shipping involves several related constructs, where the status for each construct reflects various steps in the process. Figure 5.2 summarizes this information for the basic process, and only displays those steps representing the essential touch points for updating status. Grey shading highlights the key constructs of a picking list, output order and shipment.

Figure 5.2   Life Cycles Related to the Basic Process
for Transfer Order Picking/Shipping

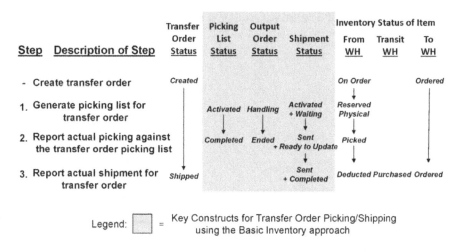

As shown in the figure, the first step will create a picking list (with line items reflecting output orders) and a corresponding shipment. It should be noted that the status for a shipment is identified by the combination of two fields termed the Shipment Status and the Physical Update Status. For example, the combination of *Activated + Waiting* indicates the shipment has been created. The right side of the figure shows the inventory status for an item on a transfer order line. At the ship-from warehouse, for example, various steps in the process will change this status from *on order* to *reserved physical, picked* and *deducted*.

Information about the related life cycles provides the foundation for explaining the reversing transactions and is covered in the next section. An extended explanation of each status was provided in the previous chapter (Section 4.10).

5.4 Reversing Transactions in the Basic Process

The ability to reverse transactions requires an understanding of the current point within the business process and the associated status of key constructs. Borrowing from the previous figure, Figure 5.3 illustrates the steps within the basic process (shown in grey text), and the various points at which you can perform reversing transactions (shown in black text). The figure also illustrates the impact of a reversing transaction on status, and the arrows indicate the resulting point in the business process. As identified by step numbers in the figure, you can reverse transactions (1X) after initially generating a picking list and (2X) after reporting actual picking.

Figure 5.3   Reversing Transactions in the Basic Process
for Transfer Order Picking/Shipping

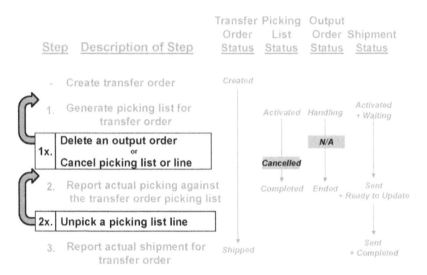

Step 1X: Reverse Transaction After Generating Picking List You can delete an output order (on the Output Order form) prior to actual picking, which automatically deletes the corresponding line on a picking list. Alternatively, you can cancel a picking list line or the entire picking list, which also deletes the corresponding output order(s). A deleted output order no longer has a status, as shown by a value of "N/A" within the figure.

Step 2X: Reverse Transaction After Actual Picking You can unpick a transaction prior to actual shipment by using the Unpick function on the Picking List Registration form. Unpicking all line items will reset the picking list status to *Activated*.

Reversing Transactions After Actual Shipment of a Transfer Order
Information cannot be corrected or cancelled after reporting actual shipment of a transfer order, and the shipment must be completely received at the ship-to warehouse. Transfer journals provide one approach for making corrections. In order to correct an over-reported quantity, for example, the shipped material must be reported as received; a transfer journal can be used to move it back.

5.5 Key Constructs for Transfer Order Picking/Shipping

The Basic Inventory approach for transfer order picking/shipping involves several key constructs in addition to the transfer order. These constructs include output orders, picking lists and shipments, which are the same constructs for sales order picking/shipping. The previous chapter provided a detailed explanation of these constructs for sales orders (Section 4.5).

One key difference between transfer orders and sales orders involves the reporting of actual shipments. You use the Posting Packing Slip form for sales orders, whereas you use the Shipment form for transfer orders. Another key difference involves the selection criteria for generating transfer order picking lists. These differences and other minor ones merit a separate explanation of the key constructs for transfer orders.

In summary, an output order represents a request for picking a transfer order line item, and provides the basis for line items on a picking list. A picking list indicates what needs to be picked, and the printed picking list serves as a turnaround document for warehouse workers. You report actual picking against the picking list. Reporting actual shipment of a transfer order updates the inventory and the financial information.

Significance of an Output Order for Transfer Order Picking An output order (also termed an Inventory Order) represents a request for picking a transfer order line item. Each output order has a system-assigned number which identifies the source information such as the transfer order, item, quantity, ship-from warehouse and ship date. When generating a picking list for a transfer order, the system automatically creates an output order for each applicable line item and assigns it to the picking list. You can subsequently view the output orders that have been assigned to a picking list. Actual picking will automatically update the output order status from the initial value of *handling* to *ended*, and you can view the inventory transactions associated with the output order.

An output order can be deleted from a picking list prior to actual picking. Deletion of all output orders assigned to a picking list will also delete the picking list itself. Generating another picking list for the transfer order will automatically create the output orders.

After generating a transfer order picking list and making changes to the transfer order, such as a quantity increase or an additional line, you can generate an additional picking list that will also automatically create output orders for the related changes.

Significance of the Picking List for a Transfer Order   A picking list indicates what needs to be picked, and the printed picking list serves as a turnaround document for warehouse workers. You report actual picking against the picking list. A transfer order will typically have a single picking list in a simple scenario, such as a transfer order with a single ship date that represents a single shipment. Different picking lists may be required when the transfer order lines have different ship dates.

Each transfer order picking list has a system-assigned identifier (also termed the picking route number), and one or more line items reflect the assignment of output orders to the picking list. The generation of a picking list reserves inventory for each transfer order line (if not already reserved), and the printed picking list identifies the reserved material. After generating a picking list, it can be viewed on the Picking List Journal form and optionally reprinted.

Several approaches can be used to generate a picking list for transfer orders. One approach involves the Release Transfer Order Picking form to view and select line items for generating picking lists. A picking list can also be generated for a single order by starting from the Transfer Order form, or you can start from the Posting Picking List form to generate picking lists for multiple orders based on selection criteria. The selection criteria about transfer orders differ considerably from the selection criteria about sales orders. The next section provides further explanation of these selection criteria about transfer orders (Section 5.6).

Significance of a Shipment for a Transfer Order Each transfer order picking list has a related shipment which the system automatically creates when you generate a picking list. A shipment has no particular significance for the Basic Inventory approach. The actual shipment of a transfer order is reported on a form labeled Shipment [for a Transfer Order].[1]

Key Forms for Transfer Order Picking/Shipping Several key forms correspond to the key constructs. A quick summary of these key forms is provided below.

◆ *Posting Picking List.* Use this form to generate and print picking lists for selected transfer order line items. Actual posting will automatically create a Picking List Journal.

◆ *Picking List Journal.* Use this form to review transfer order picking lists and to access the Picking List Registration form for a selected picking list.

◆ *Picking List Registration.* Use this form to report actual picking against a transfer order picking list.

◆ *Shipment [for a Transfer Order].* Use this form to report actual shipment for a transfer order and, optionally, close a line item when the order quantity cannot be completely shipped.

◆ *Release Transfer Order Picking.* Use this form to review a subset of transfer order line items based on selection criteria. When you release selected lines for picking, you automatically access the Posting Picking List form to generate and print the picking lists.

5.6 Major Variations for Transfer Order Picking/Shipping

The basic process for transfer order picking/shipping provides the foundation for explaining variations. The major variations include a simple inventory transaction, the selection criteria for generating picking lists, and two different approaches for generating picking lists. Another major variation involves a single-step shipment with automatic receipt.

---

[1] A shipment is not created when using the Shipment [for a Transfer Order] form as part of a simple inventory transaction, nor does it involve picking lists and output orders.

Simple Inventory Transaction for Transfer Order Picking/Shipping
The shipping clerk can bypass the use of picking lists and shipments by using a simple inventory transaction where you simply report actual shipment of the transfer order.

Picking Batch-Controlled Items   The transfer order picking list can identify reserved material for the specific batch(es) to be picked. With shelf-life items and FEFO reservation logic, for example, the reserved material reflects the inventory's expiration date. Alternatively, the reserved material can reflect a batch reservation based on the requirements for batch attributes.

Picking Serialized Items   The serial number(s) can be identified when reporting actual picking against the transfer order picking list.

Selection Criteria for Generating a Transfer Order Picking List
Several approaches can be used to generate picking lists based on selection criteria. Example selection criteria are summarized in Figure 5.4. The figure indicates the applicable constructs for each selection criteria, such as the transfer order line or header. It also highlights several selection criteria (via shading) which provide the basis for prioritizing picking/shipping activities, such as the ship date and the mode of delivery.

Generate Picking Lists Using the Release Transfer Order Picking Form   The shipping clerk uses the Release Transfer Order Picking form to view a subset of open transfer order lines based on selection criteria, and releases selected lines in order to generate picking lists. As one advantage, this form displays related information about the ability to deliver the order and the need for allocation. You can temporarily reserve the inventory for selected lines. It also displays information about other requirements for the item stemming from production or sales. As a result, it makes it easier to selectively identify which transfer lines should be released for picking.

In terms of shortcomings, the form does not display a transfer line when no inventory exists for the item, but this can be corrected via customization. A related shortcoming concerns the lack of visibility about scheduled receipts, which would be helpful when production orders (or other supply orders) will be received shortly for the items that need to be transferred.

Figure 5.4 / Example Selection Criteria for
Generating Transfer Order Picking Lists

	Field Name for a Transfer Order	Applicable Construct	
		Order Header	Order Line
Basis for Prioritizing Picking/Shipping	Ship-from Warehouse	Yes	N/A
	Mode of Delivery		N/A
	Ship Date		Yes
	Transfer Order Number		N/A
	Ship-to Warehouse		N/A
	Receive Date		Yes

Generate Picking Lists Using the Picking Workbench Approach The Picking Workbench provides an alternative approach to the generation of transfer order picking lists that reflects the wave picking concept. That is, the picking lists can be grouped together under a separate identifier (termed a picking batch) and assigned to a warehouse worker. In addition, it can suggest the appropriate box size(s) and number of boxes for packing the items when generating the picking lists.

Single Step for Transfer Order Shipment with Automatic Receipt When reporting actual shipment for a sales order, you can indicate (via the Auto Receive checkbox) that the material should be automatically reported as received at the ship-to warehouse.

5.7 Minor Variations of Transfer Order Picking/Shipping

Several minor variations apply to the basic process of transfer order picking/shipping, such as the use of delivery tolerances and safety margins. Other minor variations were identified as part of the additional steps for the basic process, such as the needed actions for warehouse management.

Impact of Delivery Tolerances on Transfer Order Picking/Shipping When delivery tolerances are acceptable, they determine how much the quantities being picked and shipped for a transfer line can differ from the ordered quantity. Over- and under-delivery tolerances (related to transfer orders) are expressed as a percentage; the values assigned to an item act as defaults for a transfer order line item. Delivery tolerances of zero percent for a transfer line mean that the shipped quantity must equal the ordered quantity. A companywide policy (embedded in the Inventory Management parameters) determines whether over- and under-deliveries will be acceptable for transfer orders.

An over-delivery tolerance applies to both the picked quantity and the shipped quantity for a transfer line. For example, the system displays an error message and prevents over-picking (beyond the over-delivery tolerance) when reporting the quantity picked, as well as over-shipping (beyond the delivery tolerance) when reporting a shipped quantity.

An under-delivery tolerance only applies to the shipped quantity for a transfer line. For example, you cannot report a shipment for an under-shipped quantity (beyond the under-delivery tolerance) in conjunction with the "close short" flag or the system will display an error message.

Modeling the Required Time for Picking/Shipping Activities Some scenarios have a significant time requirement for picking/shipping activities related to a transfer order (such as 1 or 2 days), while many others have a much shorter preparation time of minutes. A significant time requirement should be included in the supply chain model so that (1) promised ship dates will reflect the required time and (2) picking will be scheduled prior to the ship date.

◆ *Identify the Required Time for Picking/Shipping as a Safety Margin* The required time can be identified as the issue safety margin, where you define the number of days as part of the Coverage Group assigned to the item. It is normally assigned as part of the Item Coverage information for the item and ship-to warehouse, where you identify the source warehouse for planned transfer orders and also override the normal Coverage Group assigned to the item.

For example, when demands exist for an item with one day prep time, master scheduling logic will generate planned orders to arrive one day before the demand date. As another consideration, when using the Release Transfer Order Picking form to anticipate picking activities, you should release orders for picking one day prior to the ship date.

◆ *Include Required Time for Picking/Shipping in Delivery Promises* The required time (expressed as the issue safety margin, described above) can be included in delivery promises based on ATP logic, where you assign a delivery date control policy of "ATP plus issue margin" to the item as part of its default order policies for inventory. For example, when manually entering a transfer order line for an item with one day prep time, the earliest possible ship date will be one day later.

Some scenarios do not use ATP logic as the basis for delivery promises. In many of these scenarios, the required time can be modeled by the sales lead time assigned to an item as part of its default order policies for inventory.

5.8 Additional Case Studies

Case 5.1: Transfer Orders to/from a Subcontractor As part of subcontracted production, transfer orders were used to send the supplied material to the subcontractor warehouse and also transfer the finished quantities back to an internal warehouse. The actual receipt of a transfer order at the subcontractor was entered as a simple inventory transaction. A simple inventory transaction was also entered for actual shipment of a transfer order from the subcontractor.

5.9 Executive Summary

The Basic Inventory approach employs an order-based picking list and a related shipment to report transfer order fulfillment. This chapter focused on transfer order picking/shipping, and the next chapter covers transfer order receiving. This chapter started with a simple yet typical business process and explained the related life cycles, transactions, and key constructs. The basic process provided a baseline for explaining variations, such as different ways to generate picking lists.

Chapter 6

Transfer Order Receiving

The order-based approach to transfer order picking/shipping also extends to receiving. As an explanatory approach, it is easiest to start with a simple yet typical business process and explain the related life cycles, reversing transactions, and key constructs. This basic process provides a baseline for explaining variations. These topics are reflected in the following sections within the chapter:

1. Basic Process for Transfer Order Receiving
2. Additional Steps in the Basic Process
3. Life Cycles Related to the Basic Process
4. Reversing Transactions in the Basic Process
5. Key Constructs for Transfer Order Receiving
6. Variations of Transfer Order Receiving

Effective distribution planning represents a critical consideration for transfer order receiving. In order to be effective, the transfer orders should reflect S&OP game plans, a reasonable model of the supply chain, and other factors such as a manageable level of expediting. These considerations will make life easier for warehouse management.

6.1 Basic Process for Transfer Order Receiving

The basic process for transfer order receiving consists of several steps typically performed by a shipping clerk and a warehouse worker and is illustrated in Figure 6.1. The process starts with the need for reporting arrival and ends with completed receipts. This section provides an overview of the basic process and describes each step in more detail.

Figure 6.1   Basic Process for Transfer Order Receiving

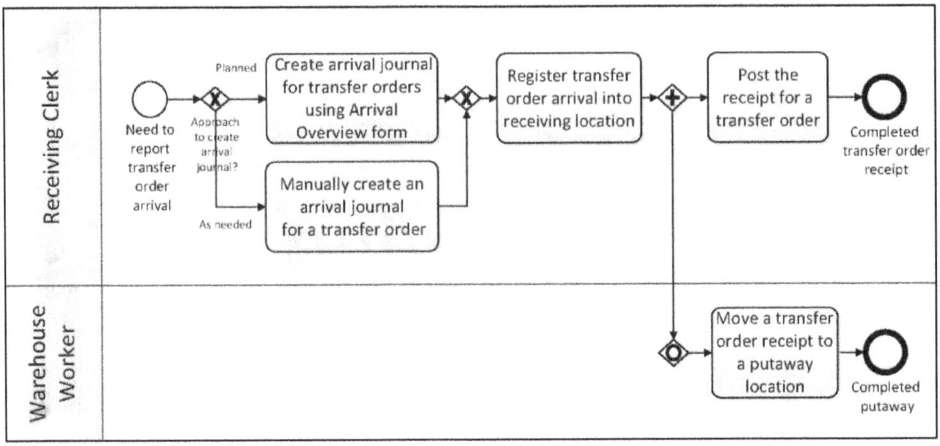

Create Arrival Journal for Transfer Orders using the Arrival Overview Form
The receiving clerk uses the Arrival Overview form to anticipate arrivals by viewing a subset of shipped transfer order line items reflecting user-specified criteria such as a ship-to location, delivery date, delivery mode, and/or transfer order number. The receiving clerk can select transfer order lines and then create an arrival journal containing the selected lines. When selecting transfer order lines, the receiving clerk can optionally analyze the estimated handling time and total weight/volume/pieces.

Manually Create an Arrival Journal for a Transfer Order
The receiving clerk uses the Arrival Journal form to manually create an arrival journal and its line items (typically to handle an unplanned receipt of a transfer order).

Register Transfer Order Arrival into a Receiving Location
The receiving clerk uses the Arrival Journal form to register the actual quantities for each journal line item and posts the arrival journal to update on-hand inventory balances. As a last step, after posting the arrival journal, the receiving clerk typically uses the Arrival Journal form to post the transfer order receipt(s) for updating financial information about the received inventory.

Post the Receipt for a Transfer Order
The receiving clerk typically posts the transfer order receipt as a related step on the Arrival Journal form (after posting the arrival journal) by accessing the Receive form It is also termed the Receive a Transfer Order form. On the Receive form, you can select the update basis for the receipt quantity—such as the registered information—and post the

receipt. The Receive form can also be accessed from the Transfer Order form (so that it inherits information from the selected order) or accessed directly (where selection criteria can be used to populate the information).

Move a Transfer Order Receipt to a Putaway Location The warehouse worker uses the Transfer Journal to report a separate putaway transaction after recording transfer order arrival or receipt, typically when the received material has been placed in a bin location representing a receiving location.

Enforce Major Steps in the Basic Process The major step of recording registration (via the arrival journal) can be enforced by the Registration Requirements policy embedded within the Item Model Group assigned to an item.

6.2 Additional Steps in the Basic Process

The basic process sometimes includes several additional steps not shown in Figure 6.1 so that the diagram does not become too complex. These steps include scrap reporting and delayed posting of the arrival journal. Other related steps about Transfer Order History and in-transit inventory were described in the previous chapter (Section 5.2).

Report a "Lost in Transit" or a Scrap Quantity When Reporting Receipt The receiving clerk can optionally identify that a scrap quantity applies to the received quantity. The scrap quantity may reflect material that has been lost in transit or scrapped material at the time of receipt. For example, a scrap quantity of 5 for the received quantity of 100 would result in an on-hand inventory of 95. The scrap quantity will automatically create two transactions to add and subtract the inventory.

Delay Posting of Arrival Journal in Order to Indicate Putaway Locations In some scenarios, the receiving clerk enters actual quantities on the arrival journal line items, and then warehouse workers enter the actual putaway locations and post the arrival journal.

6.3 Life Cycles related to the Basic Process

The basic process for transfer order receiving involves several related constructs, where the status for each construct reflects various steps in the process. Figure 6.2 summarizes this information for the basic process, and only displays those steps representing the essential touch points for updating status. Grey shading highlights the key construct of an arrival journal.

Figure 6.2   Life Cycles Related to Basic Process for
Transfer Order Receiving

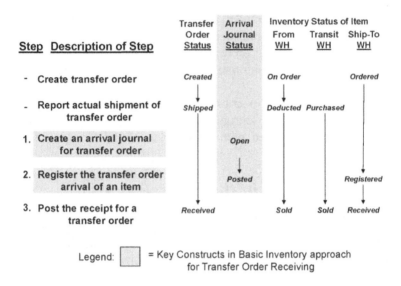

Step	Description of Step	Transfer Order Status	Arrival Journal Status	Inventory Status of Item		
				From WH	Transit WH	Ship-To WH
-	Create transfer order	Created		On Order		Ordered
-	Report actual shipment of transfer order	Shipped		Deducted	Purchased	
1.	Create an arrival journal for transfer order		Open			
2.	Register the transfer order arrival of an item		Posted			Registered
3.	Post the receipt for a transfer order	Received		Sold	Sold	Received

Legend: ▢ = Key Constructs in Basic Inventory approach
for Transfer Order Receiving

As shown in the figure, the steps will create an arrival journal (with line items reflecting transfer order lines), register the arrival (which updates inventory), and post the receipt for transfer orders (which updates financial information). The right side of the figure shows the inventory status for an item on a transfer order line. At the ship-to warehouse, for example, various steps will change this status from *ordered* to *registered* and *received.*

6.4 Reversing Transactions in the Basic Process

A reversing transaction does not apply to transfer order receipts. Transfer journals provide one approach for making corrections. In order to correct an over-reported shipped quantity, for example, the shipped material must be reported as received and then a transfer journal can be used to move it back. In addition, the entire shipped quantity must be reported as received; it cannot remain in transit. When material has been lost in transit, it can be identified as a "scrap" quantity when posting the transfer order receipt.

6.5 Key Constructs in the Basic Process

The basic process for transfer order receiving employs the key construct of an arrival journal and the related forms of an Arrival Journal and an Arrival Overview. A quick summary of these forms is provided below. The same constructs were also used and described for purchase orders (Section 5.5)

◆ *Arrival Overview.* Use this form to anticipate receiving activities and generate an arrival journal for selected transfer order lines.

◆ *Arrival Journal.* Use this form to identify the expected receipts for a transfer order and to report actual receipts. You can register the actual quantity and (when applicable) the location, batch number, and/or serial numbers for the received material. Posting the arrival journal will update on-hand inventory, but does not update financial information.

◆ *Receive [a Transfer Order]* Use the Receive form as the final step of transfer order receiving, which provides a financial update of the received inventory. It can be accessed in different ways. It can also update the line status and order status to *Received* when material has been completely received.

6.6 Variations of Transfer Order Receiving

The major variations include a simple inventory transaction and a single-step shipment; minor variations include modeling the time required for receiving activities. The use of automatically-generated quality orders does not apply to transfer order receiving.

Simple Inventory Transaction for Transfer Order Receiving   The receiving clerk can bypass the use of arrival journals by simply posting the transfer order receipt and using an update basis of the shipped quantity rather than the registered quantity.

Single Step for Transfer Order Shipment with Automatic Receipt When reporting actual shipment for a transfer order, you can indicate (via the Auto Receive checkbox) that the material should be automatically reported as received at the ship-to warehouse.

Receiving Batch-Controlled Items   There is no specialized reporting of batch numbers since they are already identified for the shipped items.

Receiving Serialized Items   There is no specialized reporting of serial numbers since they are already identified for the shipped items.

Modeling the Required Time for Transfer Order Receiving Activities
Some scenarios have a significant time requirement for receiving activities related to a transfer order (such as 1 or 2 days), while many others have a much shorter preparation time of minutes. A significant time requirement should be included in the supply chain model so that receiving will be scheduled prior to the ship date.

The required time can be identified as the receipt safety margin, where you define the number of days as part of the Coverage Group assigned to the item. It is normally assigned as part of the Item Coverage information for the item and ship-to warehouse, where you identify the source warehouse for planned transfer orders and also override the normal Coverage Group assigned to the item.

6.7 Additional Case Studies

Case 6.1: Reporting "Lost in Transit" for a Transfer Order A transfer order shipment was sometimes "lost in transit," such as an individual line item or a partial quantity of a line item. In these cases, the receiving clerk at the ship-to warehouse identified this as a separate scrap quantity when reporting the total received quantity.

Case 6.2: Updating the Transfer Order Receipt Date for Overseas Deliveries When purchasing items from suppliers in Asia, the company took ownership when the items were still at the supplier, and then used transfer orders to coordinate deliveries to their U.S. warehouses. Each transfer order represented a container, and the line items represented the container contents. The transfer order receipt date was continually updated to reflect the expected date.

6.8 Executive Summary

The order-based approach to transfer order picking/shipping also extends to receiving. This chapter started a simple yet typical business process for transfer order receiving, and explained the related life cycles, reversing transactions, and key constructs. This basic process provided a baseline for explaining variations. Several case studies illustrated the variations. These included reporting "Lost in Transit" for a transfer order and updating the transfer order receipt date for overseas deliveries.

Chapter 7

Basics of Transportation

Several basic aspects of transportation apply to sales orders, transfer orders and purchase orders regardless of the warehouse management approach. Examples include the transportation times and the significance of delivery dates used in master scheduling logic, and the charges associated with freight. Several case studies can be used to illustrate these basics of transportation. These considerations are reflected in the following sections with the chapter.

1. Transportation Basics for Sales Orders
2. Transportation Basics for Transfer Orders
3. Transportation Basics for Purchase Orders
4. Carrier Interface Information for Sales Order Shipments

An additional aspect of transportation only applies to the AX 2012 R3 version and the Basic Inventory approach to sales order shipments, where standard AX can be integrated with carrier interface information. However, this approach to carrier interface information was deprecated in the new Dynamics AX, and replaced by the advanced transportation management capabilities. It is included here for the sake of completeness.

7.1 Transportation Basics for Sales Orders

The transportation basics include sales order dates for shipment and delivery, the transportation time to a customer, the sales order promise dates, the need for expediting a sales order shipment, the sales order charges for freight/handling, and shipping documents such as a bill of lading.

Sales Order Dates for Shipment and Delivery A sales order header has a requested ship date and a requested delivery date, where the difference represents the transportation time (termed transport days) between the ship-from warehouse and the delivery address. It also has a confirmed ship date and confirmed receipt date. The assignments of these dates are affected by the delivery date control policy assigned to the sales order header, which can enforce basic rules about applicable calendars (for the ship-from warehouse, the customer, and the mode of delivery), the expected transportation time to the customer address, and order entry deadlines.

These dates within the sales order header can be inherited by the sales lines, and changes in the header dates can optionally update information for the sales lines. However, the dates for a line item are also subject to the delivery date control policy for the line item (such as ATP logic). This policy can enforce the above-mentioned rules. It is inherited from the item and can be overridden. The confirmed ship date for a sales line (if specified) will drive picking/shipping activities and master scheduling logic, otherwise the requested ship date will be used.

Transportation Time to a Customer   The number of days for expected transportation time can be specified for different combinations of the ship-from warehouse, the delivery address characteristics (such as the country, state, county, or ZIP code), and the mode of delivery (such as air or truck). The mode of delivery and address can be assigned to the sales order header and inherited by the line items, or specified for each line item if needed.

A calendar can be assigned to various modes of delivery for the ship-from warehouse, where the calendar determines the working days when items can be transported. For example, a truck route may only occur on Thursdays.

The mode of delivery can be inherited from a sales agreement. For example, it can be inherited by releasing a sales order from a sales agreement or by manually creating a sales order linked to a sales agreement.

Sales Order Promise Dates for Shipment and Delivery   The delivery date control policy for a sales order line can enforce several basic rules related to transportation when making delivery promises. These rules include the calendar of working days at the ship-from warehouse and at the customer receiving point, the calendar assigned to the mode of delivery, the transportation time to the customer, and the sales lead time for preparing items for shipment. These rules apply to the automatic assignment of dates when initially entering a sales order header or line, and when manually entering a date. A policy of "none" means that the basic rules will be ignored so that promise dates and transportation considerations can be unrealistic.

Need for Expediting a Sales Order Shipment   The need for expediting can be identified on a sales order header and its line items, such as the expedited shipment flag and an expedite code. These can be used for generating sales order picking lists, as described in a previous chapter (Section 4.7).

Sales Order Charges for Freight/Handling   The charges related to freight and handling can be manually assigned to a sales order, either as order-level charges or line item charges or both. A user-defined Charges Code identifies each type of charge and its related ledger account. The charges can be expressed as a fixed amount, an amount per piece, or a percentage of value. A fixed amount (for an order-level charge) needs to be allocated to the lines.

Some sales environments involve predefined agreements about charges, such as freight or handling charges for selected items or customers. An agreement about charges can be embedded in the sales price trade agreement information, or they can be specified separately as *auto charges*. These auto charges can be applied to an entire sales order or to individual line items, and expressed as a fixed amount, an amount per piece, or a percentage of value.

◆ *Order-Level Charges.* Charge agreements related to the entire sales order can be defined for a single customer, all customers or a group of customers, (identified by the *Customer Charges Group* assigned to relevant customers). Examples of an order-level charge include order preparation costs for selected customers.

◆ *Line Item Charges.* Charge agreements related to the sales order line item can be defined by customer and item, such as charges for a single item, all items, or a group of items (identified by the Item Charges group assigned to relevant salable items).[1] Examples of a line item charge include a setup fee for producing selected items for a customer.

Bill of Lading and Other Shipping Documents   A bill of lading represents one of several shipping documents that may be needed for a sales order shipment. A bill of lading can be automatically created by posting a sales order packing list or invoice. Some information pertaining to the system-assigned bill of lading identifier is automatically updated, such as the customer, sales order number, delivery address, and the shipped items and quantities. The bill of lading information reflects the item number and description. Other bill of lading information must be manually maintained, including each package type (such as carton), quantity and weight. Use the bill of lading form for data maintenance

---

[1] Two policies (embedded within the A/R parameters) indicate whether the system recognizes auto charges for the entire order and for line items.

and document printing. A bill of lading can be manually created to support other types of shipments (such as office furniture), or to support a master bill of lading (such as shipments to a freight forwarder). After creating a bill of lading identifier, for example, you explicitly designate it as a master bill of lading and also assign the identifier to individual bills of lading associated with it.

Case 7.1: Identify Truck Routes for Regional Customer Deliveries A manufacturing/distribution company employed internal trucks for making regional customer deliveries, and identified the four variations of truck routes as different modes of delivery. For example, one truck route applied to northern customer locations with M-W-F deliveries and another truck route applied to the southern locations with T-R-S deliveries. The calendar assigned to each mode of delivery identified these periodic deliveries. A mode of delivery (aka truck route) was also assigned to each customer so that it would be inherited by sales orders.

Case 7.2: Charges for Faster-than-Normal Delivery on Sales Orders A distribution company employed several types of rules-based pricing when selling their products to retailers. The approaches included a surcharge for a small order and discounts for a large order (based on total order value), as well as discount percentages and supplementary items based on total quantity ordered for different items within a product line. A miscellaneous charge was added to items requiring faster-than-normal delivery lead time.

Case 7.3: Using the Basic Inventory Approach and Still Use Advanced Transportation Capabilities The capabilities within advanced transportation management were deemed critical for a company intending to use the basic approach to warehouse management. They were considering the option proposed in a blog about "using transportation management without the new warehouse management module." The proposed option employed items that were not WMS-enabled, but were still assigned the policy to "use transportation management processes." This approach would allow them to use the Load Planning Workbench to create a load for sales orders and then use the rating and routing capabilities.

7.2 Transportation Basics for Transfer Orders

The transportation basics include transfer order dates for shipment and delivery, the transportation time between warehouses, and the transfer order promise dates.

Transfer Order Dates for Shipment and Delivery The transfer order header specifies a shipment date and receipt date, along with the ship-from and ship-to site/warehouses and a mode of delivery such as air or truck. The difference between the two dates reflects the expected transportation time (expressed in days) between the two locations.

The assignments of these dates are affected by the delivery date control policy assigned to the transfer order header, which can enforce basic rules such as the working calendar for both warehouses, the calendar for the delivery mode, and the expected transportation time between a pair of warehouses.

These dates and delivery mode within the transfer order header can be inherited by the line items, and changes in the header can optionally update information for the line items. However, the dates for a line item are also subject to the delivery date control policy for the line item (such as ATP logic). This policy can enforce the above-mentioned rules. It is inherited from the item and can be overridden. The ship date for a transfer line will drive picking/shipping activities and master scheduling logic.

Transportation Time Between Warehouses You define the transportation time between a pair of warehouses using the Transport form, and the time can vary by delivery mode.

Transfer Order Promise Dates for Shipment and Delivery The delivery date control policy for a transfer line can enforce several basic rules related to transportation when making delivery promises. These rules include the calendar of working days at the ship-from warehouse and at the ship-to warehouse, the calendar assigned to the mode of delivery, the transportation time between the warehouse, and the sales lead time for preparing items for shipment. These rules apply to the automatic assignment of dates when initially entering a transfer order header or line, and when manually entering a date. A policy of "none" means that the basic rules will be ignored so that promise dates and transportation considerations can be unrealistic.

Case 7.4: Transportation Constraints about Transfer Orders to/from a Subcontractor An electronics manufacturer located in the United States sent supplied material via truck to its subcontractor in Mexico, and the completed subassembly was sent back via truck to its US location. The weekly truck schedules to and from Mexico were identified as two different modes of delivery, and the associated calendars identified which days the truck departed and an estimated transportation time (expressed in days). The contents of a given truck were identified as line items on a transfer order. These transportation constraints were used by master scheduling logic to suggest appropriate dates and quantities for planned transfer orders and subcontracted production orders, and coordinate the supply chain accordingly. This approach provided full visibility of inventory at the subcontractor location and in transit.

Case 7.5: Coordinate Transportation for Asian Subcontractors The office furniture products for a US distribution company were produced by a subcontractor in Taiwan using supplied material from vendors located in nearby countries, and the finished goods were shipped monthly from Taiwan in a container. A transfer order represented each container and the line items identified its contents. Its shipment and delivery dates reflected the 4-week transportation time to the US distribution center. The purchase orders for supplied material were delivered to the Taiwan subcontractor. Each subcontracted production order reflected the monthly shipment intervals, and finished quantities were received at the subcontractor site prior to reporting transfer order shipment. These transportation considerations were used by master scheduling logic to suggest appropriate dates and quantities for planned transfer orders as well as the related orders for subcontracted production and the purchase orders for supplied material.

7.3 Transportation Basics for Purchase Orders

The transportation basics include the significance of a confirmed delivery date, the mode of delivery for a purchase order, and purchase order charges for freight/handling.

Significance of a Confirmed Delivery Date Each purchase order line (and a line within a delivery schedule) has a delivery date and a separate "confirmed" delivery date. The confirmed delivery date is initially blank, and should be updated to reflect actual confirmation from the vendor or the carrier. If specified, the confirmed date will be used for anticipating warehouse receipts and by master scheduling logic—otherwise the delivery date will be used. For example, if the confirmed delivery date reflects a projected delay, master scheduling logic can identify (via futures messages) the impact of the projected delay in meeting a sales order shipment date.

Changing the delivery date within a purchase order header can optionally update the delivery date for every line (with a prompt or without a prompt), as defined by a companywide policy (embedded in the A/P parameters).

Mode of Delivery for a Purchase Order The mode of delivery and address can be assigned to the purchase order header and inherited by the line items, or specified for each line item if needed. A calendar can be assigned to various modes of delivery for the ship-to warehouse, where the calendar determines the working days when items can be transported.

The mode of delivery can be inherited from a purchase agreement. For example, it can be inherited by releasing a purchase order from a purchase agreement, by manually creating a purchase order linked to a purchase agreement, or by firming planned purchase orders with grouping by purchase agreement.

Purchase Order Charges for Freight/Handling The charges related to freight and handling can be manually assigned to a purchase order, either as order-level charges or line item charges or both. A user-defined Charges Code identifies each type of charge and its related ledger account. The charges can be expressed as a fixed amount, an amount per piece, or a percentage of value. A fixed amount (for an order-level charge) needs to be allocated to the lines.

Some purchase environments involve predefined agreements about charges, such as handling or freight charges for selected items or vendors. These charges can be embedded in the purchase price trade agreement information, or they can be specified separately as *auto charges*. These auto charges can be applied to an entire purchase order or to individual line items, and expressed as a fixed amount, an amount per piece, or a percentage of value.

♦ *Order-Level Charges.* Charge agreements related to the entire purchase order can be defined for a single vendor, all vendors or a group of vendors (identified by the *Vendor Charges Group* assigned to relevant vendors). Examples of an order-level charge include order preparation costs for selected vendors.

♦ *Line Item Charges.* Charges related to the purchase order line item can be defined by vendor and item, such as charges for a single item, all items, or a group of items (identified by the Item Charges Group assigned to relevant purchased items). Examples of a line item charge include a setup fee for purchasing selected items from a vendor.

Case 7.6: Freight Charges for a Purchase Order and its Invoice At a manufacturing company, the purchasing agent manually assigned the expected freight charges on a purchase order header. The charges consist of a freight charge code and an expected amount (expressed as a fixed amount) which was allocated to the purchase order lines. When entering a vendor's invoice for the purchase order, the accounts payable clerk reviewed the expected freight charges and entered the actual fright charges if different. The accounts payable clerk reviewed a comparison of actual versus expected freight charges, which highlighted discrepancies exceeding a predefined tolerance. The clerk needed to approve a vendor's invoice when a charges discrepancy exceeded the predefined tolerance.

7.4 Carrier Interface Information for Sales Order Shipments

Some scenarios using AX 2012 R3 and the Basic Inventory Approach need integration with shipping carrier software.[2] Standard AX functionality only supports this integration for sales order shipments. When you post a sales order packing slip, information about the shipment can be automatically transferred to the shipping carrier software—such as Kewill ClipperShip, UPS WorldShip, and FedEx Ship Manager—and the resulting information about freight charges and tracking numbers can be transferred back to the sales order. This helps eliminate manual entry and improve tracking visibility.

The integration with shipping carrier software requires considerable setup information, including the definition of carrier companies, the applicable charge codes, delivery modes and terms of delivery for each shipping carrier, and default shipping carrier information for each customer. A detailed explanation falls outside the book's scope.

7.5 Executive Summary

Several basic aspects of transportation apply to sales orders, transfer orders and purchase orders regardless of the warehouse management approach. Examples include the transportation times and the significance of delivery dates used in master scheduling logic, and the charges associated with freight. These transportation basics reflect key aspects of how a company models and manages its supply chain, especially in terms of the detailed game plans that everybody is working to. The additional aspects of any transportation management capabilities need to support these detailed game plans or update the details if they change—such as changing a ship date or a delivery date.

These case studies identified several transportation issues, including truck routes for regional customer deliveries, transportation constraints about transfer orders to/from a subcontractor, coordination of transportation for Asian subcontractors, and freight charges for a purchase order and its invoice.

---

[2] This approach to carrier interface information is not supported in the new Dynamics AX. It is included here for the sake of completeness.

Chapter 8

Quality Management Considerations

The concerns of quality management often extend across almost every aspect of a manufacturing/distribution business. This broad viewpoint ranges from the definition of item and product structure information through sourcing purchased material, actual production, sales shipments, and returns. A narrower viewpoint focuses on several aspects of unique functionality for quality management, especially those related to warehouse management. This narrower viewpoint includes inventory blocking approaches, variations of an inspection approach, and the use of quarantine orders. The chapter consists of the following sections.

1. Summary of Inventory Blocking Approaches
2. Variations of an Inspection Approach
3. Quarantine Orders

Many other quality management considerations are covered in the complete book about warehouse management. Examples include the use of quality orders, the use of cases to report quality problems, the assignment of a disposition code to customer returns, the impact of holds and stopped flags, the use of nonconformance reports, the management of hazardous materials, and the coordination of quality-related activities.

8.1 Summary of Inventory Blocking Approaches

Inventory blocking represents a key tool for quality management, such as preventing usage and indicating the need for inspection. There are three basic sources or approaches for inventory blocking -- labeled Inventory Status, Quality Order and Manual. Each approach results in an entry on the Inventory Blocking form along with information about the source of blocking. This information can act as a coordination tool for quality management.

One approach employs a blocked value for Inventory Status, as described in a previous chapter (Section 2.2). The second approach employs quality orders, and often works in conjunction with the values of Inventory Status. The third approach involves manual assignment of inventory blocking. The three approaches differ in how the inventory blocking is created and removed, their impact on master scheduling logic, and their allowable transactions. The three approaches are summarized in Figure 8.1 and described below.

Figure 8.1 Summary of Inventory Blocking Approaches

Considerations about Blocking	Type of Inventory Blocking		
	Inventory Status	Quality Order	Manual
Create blocking for the specified inventory of item	Assign a blocked value for Inventory Status	Create a quality order with full blocking	Manually assign inventory blocking
Ability to assign blocking at time of order receipt	Yes	Yes	No
Remove blocking	Change a blocked value for Inventory Status	Delete or complete the quality order	Delete manual assignment of inventory blocking
Impact of blocked inventory on master scheduling logic	Non-nettable	Nettable on expected date	Non-nettable or Nettable on expected date
Allowable transactions for the blocked inventory	Move, adjustment out Cycle count Return to vendor Create quality order	None	None
Description for blocking	None	Yes	Yes
Note/document for blocking	None	Yes	Yes
Additional considerations	Assign to subset of a batch number Different ways to change value of Inventory Status	Block just sample quantity Impact next steps for order Destructive testing Update Inventory Status or Batch Disposition Code	Assign to subset of a batch number

Inventory Blocking based on a blocked value of Inventory Status

This approach reflects a blocked value for Inventory Status which can be assigned at the time of order receipt. The blocking can be viewed on the Inventory Blocking form, and it can only be removed by changing it to a non-blocked value. The inventory is treated as unusable and non-nettable by master scheduling logic. The blocking prevents most inventory transactions with the exception of moves, adjustments, cycle counts, returns to vendor and creation of a quality order. A blocked value can be changed by a quality order or changed directly (via a client or mobile device transaction). A blocked value can also be assigned to a subset of a batch number or to a specific serial number.

Inventory Blocking based on a Quality Order This approach reflects a quality order with "full blocking" as part of the policies for item sampling. A quality order can be manually created for the specified inventory of an item, including inventory that has already been assigned a blocked value for Inventory Status. Alternatively, an item's quality order can be automatically created based on policies defined on the Quality Association form, such as automatic creation as a result of reporting purchase order arrival or the finished quantity for a production order. Using the Inventory Blocking form, you can optionally define a description and/or notes about blocking related to a quality order.

With full blocking, the inventory associated with a quality order is treated by master scheduling logic as nettable with an expected availability date. This expected outcome is indicated by the automatically-assigned Expected Receipts checkbox. The expected date inherits the creation date and can be manually changed. However, the blocking prevents all inventory transactions.

Blocking based on a quality order has several additional considerations shown at the bottom of Figure 8.1. For example, blocking can just apply to a small sample quantity, and a quality order can be used to update the value of Inventory Status or the Batch Disposition Code.

Inventory Blocking based on Manual Assignment This approach reflects a manual assignment of inventory blocking to existing inventory. It can only be created and deleted on the Inventory Blocking form, and you can optionally define a description and/or notes about the manual blocking. When you create manual blocking, you can indicate the expected outcome as non-nettable or as nettable with an expected availability date. You indicate the expected outcome via an Expected Receipts checkbox. The expected date inherits the creation date and can be manually changed. Manual blocking prevents all inventory transactions. For example, the manual blocking must be removed in order to report the inventory as scrapped. Manual blocking can also be assigned to a subset of a batch number or to a specific serial number.

8.2 Variations of an Inspection Approach

Different approaches to inspection reflect several factors. Some of these factors include the different values for Inventory Status, and the different roles and ways for reporting a change in value. Other differences reflect the use of a separate QC location and the differences between purchased versus manufactured items. This section covers several variations of inspection approaches.

Variations of Inspection Using Inventory Status   The value for Inventory Status provides one basis for identifying the need for inspection as well as the results of inspection.   For example, for purchase order arrivals, the value can be assigned by a non-QC person such as a receiving clerk (Case 3.4), or by a quality control clerk based on the test results for a quality order (Case 8.1).

Variations of Inspection Using Batch Disposition Codes   The batch disposition code provides one basis for identifying the results of inspection for a batch-controlled item.   The value is typically assigned by a quality control clerk based on the test results for a quality order for purchase order arrivals or production order receipts.

Variations of Inspection Using a Separate QC Area   Material may be placed in a separate QC location until inspection results have been reported.   The good material can then be put away into a stocking location.

Variations of Inspection Using a Quarantine Order   A quarantine order provides one basis for identifying the need for inspection and the results of inspection, as described in a subsequent section (Section 8.2).   This approach employs the concept of a separate QC location within a quarantine warehouse, although it also supports "in place" inspection.

Other Variations of Reporting Inspection Results   Other variations include reporting of quality order results after putaway, and reporting delayed test results for a quality order.

8.3 Quarantine Orders

A quarantine order represents one of the inspection approaches, and it only works for the basic approach to warehouse management. It involves placement of an item's inventory into a quarantine warehouse and location, which prevents usage until the quarantine order has been ended. Its supports scrap reporting of rejected material. For useable material, it supports an expected availability date and optional putaway to a normal warehouse and location.

A quarantine order can be created using several different approaches. For example, it can be manually created, or automatically created from an arrival journal or for a failed quality order. These different starting points and the typical business process for a quarantine order are illustrated in Figure 8.2 and described below.

Figure 8.2   Process a Quarantine Order

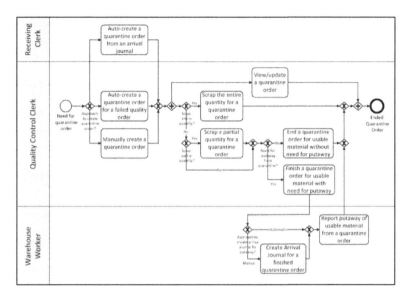

The setup information for handling a quarantine order includes the definition of a quarantine warehouse (and associated bin locations), and assignment of this quarantine warehouse to the corresponding main warehouse.   The locations within a quarantine warehouse can reflect QC-specific locations when inspection involves a separate QC area.   They can also mirror some of the locations in a normal warehouse when inspection of inventory occurs in place.

Auto-Create a Quarantine Order From an Arrival Journal   When registering purchase order arrival using an arrival journal, the receiving clerk can identify the need for a quarantine order on a journal line.   The need for a quarantine order can also be inherited from an item-specific policy (embedded within the Item Model Group assigned to the item).

Auto-Create a Quarantine Order for a Failed Quality Order   When reporting validation of test results for a quality order, the quality control clerk can specify that a quarantine order should be automatically created upon validation failure of the test results.   This will automatically move the material to the quarantine warehouse and a related bin location, and prevent usage until the quarantine order has been processed.

As part of the setup information, you can define a policy for creating a quarantine order upon validation failure (within the Quality Association information for an item) which acts as the default when validating a quality order.

Manually Create a Quarantine Order   The quality control clerk can manually create a quarantine order for an item's inventory.

View/Update a Quarantine Order   The quality control clerk can view quarantine orders and their status, and also update the information. For example, the quality control clerk can assign an expected availability date and optionally split the quantity to create an additional quarantine order for reporting different results. The newly-created quarantine order has a status of Created, and requires an additional step for updating the status to Started. Other updates include scrap reporting and possible transfers to putaway locations, as described in subsequent steps.

Scrap the Entire Quantity for a Quarantine Order   The quality control clerk determines the item is not usable and scraps the entire quantity, which removes the quantity from inventory and charges the Inventory Loss account. It also updates the quarantine order status to Ended.

Scrap a Partial Quantity for a Quarantine Order   The quality control clerk determines that a partial quantity is not usable and must be scrapped, which removes the quantity from inventory and charges the Inventory Loss account.

End a Quarantine Order for Usable Material Without Need for Putaway   For usable material that does not require putaway, the quality control clerk reports a quarantine order as Ended. The inventory remains in the same location (within a main warehouse and location) that reflects initial creation of the quarantine order.

Finish a Quarantine Order for Usable Material With Need for Putaway   For usable material requiring putaway, the quality control clerk changes the quarantine order status to Reported as Finished and designates the approach for creating an arrival journal to handle putaway. An arrival journal name can be specified (to indicate an automatic creation approach) or left blank (to indicate a manual creation approach).

Create an Arrival Journal for a Finished Quarantine Order   The warehouse worker creates an arrival journal for a finished Quarantine Order in order to support putaway of the usable material. This arrival journal can be created manually or created from the Arrival Overview form.

Perform Putaway of Usable Material From a Quarantine Order The warehouse worker uses the arrival journal (associated with the Quarantine Order) to move the material from the quarantine location to the desired put-away location. Posting the arrival journal automatically updates the quarantine order status to Ended.

8.4 Additional Case Studies

Case 8.1: Assign Inventory Status based on Test Results for a Quality Order

The warehouse manager and quality manager at a manufacturing company were considering options for identifying needed action about received material based on the test results for a quality order. One approach involved the user-defined values for Inventory Status with possible values of *Good, To-Be-Scrapped, Return-to-Vendor and Needs-Rework*. The default value for inventory status was typically identified as *Good* on purchase order lines.

The proposed approach employs automatically-created quality orders for purchase order arrivals, where the quality control clerk identifies the applicable value when a failed validation occurs. In addition, the approach identifies an accounts payable clerk as responsible for posting of product receipts so that the quality order results can be considered. The two managers prepared a diagram (Figure 8.3) of the proposed business process.

The receiving inspection process starts with registration of a purchase order arrival into a receiving location which automatically generates a quality order, and it has multiple end points reflecting the test results of the quality order. The inventory remains in the receiving location until completion of the quality order. The process consists of several steps performed by different roles, and three of these steps merit further explanation.

◆ *Process a Quality Order for a Purchase Order Arrival.* The activities of quality control clerks are coordinated based on a review of open quality orders, using either the Quality Orders form or the Inventory Blocking form. When reporting test results for a given quality order, the quality control clerk indicates the applicable Inventory Status for validation failure, such as *Scrap, Return-to-Vendor,* or *Needs-Rework.* Validation automatically updates the Inventory Status of the received material.

Figure 8.3   Receiving Inspection Using a Quality Order
and Inventory Status

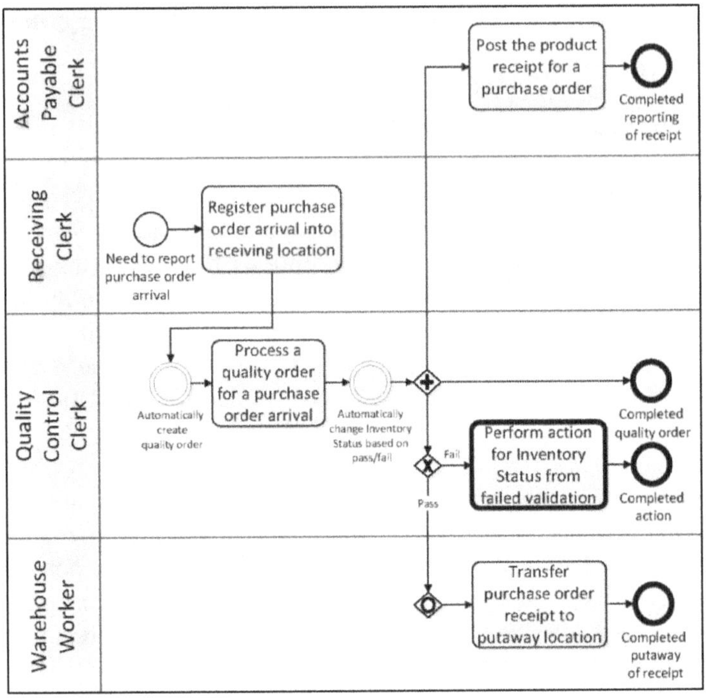

◆ *Perform Action for Inventory Status from Failed Validation.* The quality control clerk reports an inventory adjustment for material assigned an Inventory Status of *Scrap*. The production planner creates a rework order for material with a *Needs-Rework* status. The accounts payable clerk creates a purchase order return for material with a *Return-to-Vendor* status. For material with a *Good* status, the warehouse worker reports a transfer from the receiving location to a stocking location.

◆ *Post the Product Receipt for a Purchase Order.* The accounts payable clerk posts the product receipt after completion of the quality order. In this way, the posting can be blocked until completion, and a validation failure will be communicated (via a message) when posting the product receipt.

Case 8.2: Indicate Need for a Quarantine Order When Reporting a Purchase Order Arrival
The receiving clerks at a manufacturing/distribution company could identify the need for a quarantine order when reporting purchase order arrival via the arrival journal. This resulted in an automatically-generated

quarantine order in order to communicate the need for further inspection. The receiving clerks also placed the inventory in a bin location within the quarantine warehouse.

8.5 Executive Summary

This chapter covered several quality management considerations for warehouse management. As a starting point, it explained the use of inventory blocking to prevent usage or indicate the need for inspection. It also covered several variations of inspection approaches, including the use of quarantine orders.

Chapter 9

Summary

This book focused on how Microsoft Dynamics AX provides an integrated ERP system to support the basic approach to warehouse management in manufacturing and distribution businesses. The targeted reader consists of warehouse management professionals that need to initially learn AX. It provided an overview of the essential business processes and capabilities, and covered the embedded conceptual models and business processes that ultimately shape your vocabulary for describing system usage.

The sequence of topics started with the fundamentals of the basic approach to warehouse management. This included the significance of Inventory Status, the definition of a warehouse and its bin locations, and the basic inventory transactions such as adjustments and transfers. Subsequent chapters covered several types of warehouse-related transactions, including purchase order receiving, sales order picking/shipping, and transfer order picking/shipping and receiving. These transactions also involve several considerations about transportation and quality management. For each type of transaction, the explanation covered a basic model of the business process, the related constructs and their life cycles, the reversing transactions, and the major variations. The basic model provided a baseline for explaining these variations, thereby supporting a "+1" learning approach.

This Essential Guide book represents an abbreviated version of my complete book for "Warehouse Management using Microsoft Dynamics AX: 2016 Edition". The Essential Guide focused on topics that apply to both distribution and manufacturing, but skimmed over the manufacturing-related topics due to book length considerations. These topics are covered in the complete book.

The book contents covered the two major options currently available for using AX, which can be labeled "Dynamics AX 2012 R3" and the "new Dynamics AX". The two options provide the same supply chain management functionality with some slight differences, so that the book contents apply to both options.

The book identified the slight differences such as the variations in user experience and the workspace capabilities.

Concluding Remarks   When learning any ERP software package, it is important to understand its underlying conceptual models and how it supports basic business processes and their variations. It is easy to get bogged down in the navigational details. This book summarized how Microsoft Dynamics AX can support the basic approach to warehouse management in manufacturing and distribution businesses, and addressed the learning objectives for those new to AX.

Appendix A
Scope of Book Topics
and Prior Research

The book focuses on basic warehouse management within the larger context of supply chain management, especially for distribution and manufacturing companies. This focus guided the prior research and the scope of book topics.

Prior Research Several steps of prior research were undertaken to understand the requirements in manufacturing/distribution for warehouse and supply chain management, and the AX functionality to support those requirements. With respect to AX 2012 R3 (as well as previous AX versions), these steps included participation in training classes, webinars, and conference sessions; reviews of the existing training materials, e-learning lessons, user documentation and sales demo materials; reviews of blogs and articles; discussions with users, development personnel, and field consultants; and hands-on testing for thousands of use cases that reflected common requirements in manufacturing and distribution. With few exceptions, only those capabilities personally tested and proven were included in the book contents. [1] The same approach was also undertaken for my previous books about Dynamics AX. The discussions with experienced field consultants helped identify the dominant business practices at current users. On-going opportunities to consult with current users have supplemented this understanding.

The prior research concerning the new Dynamics AX has been following similar steps. This included participation in pre-release webinars and conferences, discussions with leading experts and Microsoft team members, reading the currently available information, and hands-on testing of hundreds of use cases.

---

[1] The prior research and hands-on testing for AX 2012 R3 reflect the software capabilities through the CU9 release.

These same use cases were previously tested for AX 2012 R3, thereby supporting a comparative analysis of the two options. The book contents reflect my prior research up until the beginning of the year 2016.

The prior research about warehouse management within the larger context of supply chain management included my consulting and teaching experiences with manufacturing and distribution firms across the past three decades. These experiences included responses to numerous RFPs (requests for proposal) for an ERP system, face-to-face consulting engagements with several hundred firms, and teaching executive seminars, APICS certification classes, MBA courses, and user group sessions. However, there are many aspects of warehouse management – both technical and managerial – that fall outside the book's scope and my current level of expertise/experience to explain them.

Scope of Book Topics   The book topics focus on the basic approach to warehouse management within Dynamics AX, and the selection of book topics was shaped by several factors. First, the selected topics excluded the integrated accounting applications except for key intersection points with warehouse management. Second, several topics were excluded because of book length considerations -- such as warehouse management transactions for manufacturing, project-oriented operations, service-oriented operations and retail operations – although they are mentioned in several places. Many of the topics related to manufacturing (such as production order picking and receiving) and quality are covered in my complete book about warehouse management. Third, a few topics were excluded because they could not be personally tested and proven within the budgeted time. The book length considerations precluded screen shots.

Contributions to the AX Body of Knowledge   The body of knowledge related to Microsoft Dynamics AX consists of several levels and components. The foundation level consists of the software, documentation and training materials provided by Microsoft. Additional contributions to the AX body of knowledge build on this foundation. In terms of the book's contributions, I have attempted to summarize the relevant information with an integrative viewpoint of how the whole system fits together to support basic warehouse management in manufacturing and distribution businesses. The book explains the embedded conceptual models and business processes for running these businesses.

List of Figures

List of Cases

About the Author

Scott Hamilton has specialized in SCM/ERP information systems for three decades and consulted globally with several hundred manufacturing/distribution companies. His publications include multiple books about SCM using Dynamics AX as well as two textbooks about SCM/ERP, and his books have been translated into Russian and Chinese. His regular column "The AX Solution Architect" is published in MSDynamicsWorld.com. Scott has been a frequent speaker at Microsoft and AXUG events around the world, and a multi-year winner of the rarely-given Microsoft MVP award for AX. He earned a doctorate in information systems specializing in manufacturing and taught SCM/ERP as an MBA professor at several leading universities in North America, Europe and the Pacific Rim. He lives in Minnesota, a place where people still build ice castles.

About UXC Eclipse

Scott Hamilton has become the "go to" authority on Microsoft Dynamics AX in the manufacturing space. His books provide valuable insights into the market place we serve, which gives us all the opportunity to expand our thinking and see beyond the software features and functions.

UXC Eclipse is widely recognized as a global leader in industry solutions built on the Dynamics AX platform. We have a depth of experience across the horizontal global ERP market with specific focus on industry solutions for Retail, Wholesale and Distribution, Manufacturing and the surrounding supply chain.

We help organizations streamline their business and operational processes to bring the best from their organizational experience to the best of our Dynamics AX solutions; the result is 'win-win'. From their Dynamics AX solutions, our customers realize operational efficiencies, improve business performance and heighten their supply chain collaboration. At UXC Eclipse we use a combination of old-fashioned service with ISO-9001 accredited quality systems and controls to ensure our implementations deliver to our customers' expectations – on time and on budget. Our happy customers are the true indication of our success. With a global team of over 650 people, some 2,700 customer sites rely on UXC Eclipse for their project implementation services and everyday support.

We trust you find this book to be a useful insight into Microsoft Dynamics AX. If UXC Eclipse can be of service on your supply chain journey, then please get in touch with us at _www.uxceclipse.com_

Bradley Stroop
Chief Executive Officer
UXC Eclipse Group

Made in the USA
Middletown, DE
23 December 2019

81868820R00066